BeLonging

Also by Peter Selby and published by SPCK

Liberating God: Private Care and Public Struggle
(New Library of Pastoral Care)

PETER SELBY

BeLonging

Challenge to a Tribal Church

First published in Great Britain 1991
SPCK
Holy Trinity Church
Marylebone Road
London NW1 4DU

British Library Cataloguing in Publication Data

Selby, Peter
Belonging.
1. Christian church
I. Title
260

ISBN 0–281–04506–2

Phototypeset by Input Typesetting Ltd, London
Printed in Great Britain by
The Longdunn Press Ltd, Bristol

Contents

Preface

'What kind of Church would support the sort of pastoral care you describe?' I found that question, asked by a reader of my *Liberating God: Private Care and Public Struggle*, stayed with me. I am grateful for three particular sources of stimulation over the succeeding years which have led to this book.

An unpublished paper by Dr Harvey Guthrie, delivered some years ago at a conference on the ordination of women, seemed to provide a framework for an understanding of the Church which would enable particular debates to be considered in a wider framework. I am grateful to him for permission to use it (see particularly Chapter 3), and for the spacious vision of Christian ministry which he has represented for me ever since I was a student of his some twenty-five years ago.

For the last six years I have been a recipient, for the second time in my life, of the demanding and stimulating atmosphere of the Church of England in the diocese of Southwark. The concerns pursued in this book are there matters of daily engagement. I am grateful to those colleagues who made possible a period of study leave during which most of it was written. My particular thanks are due to Bishops Ronnie Bowlby, Peter Hall and Wilfred Wood for what I have learned from them; they bear no responsibility for the particular lines of my argument, but I hope they will recognize here some of the themes and ideas with which we struggled during the studies we undertook together in the Epistle to the Galatians.

On her return from the General Synod debate on sexual morality in November 1987, Jan, my wife, wrote to a church newspaper a letter, unpublished until now (see pages 49–50), which seemed to me to capture in a most profound and direct way the betrayal of mission and charity in both the substance and manner of that debate. Apart from its contribution to the theme of the book, that letter is representative of Jan's part in the experience and reflection which we share.

Peter Selby
Southfields, London
Pentecost 1990

1

Longing and Belonging

It is human to want things to be different. You can feel that life is being quite good to you, and at the same time want something more. In fact feeling that life is being good to you can make you even more aware of how things could be and are not. 'How marvellous' and 'if only' are very close together.

Both feelings are also very close to the heart of religion. In faith you contemplate the world about you, and you are filled with a sense of thankfulness, of delight in the rich variety and beauty of the universe; so you perceive it as *creation*, the work of God whose love and wisdom overflowed into an infinity of creatures, intended for relationship with God and each other.

In the same instant you perceive scars which mar its beauty, and suddenly you are aware of the ruptured relationships, the exploitation and the imposed ugliness. So you perceive the universe as *fallen* and long for it to come to wholeness and attain to the beauty and order that you sense are intended for it. Faith also perceives, between the way things are and the way they are meant to be, wrong human choices — the failure to understand or to carry out what our intelligence and our freedom call for.

The link between delight and longing appears as a general human experience; it is almost always there in religious faith also. Those who believe in God come to see both delight and longing not just as a feature of their own inner landscape, but as an aspect of the God in whom they believe. Delight and longing are, in that sense, embedded in the heart of life's meaning and direction, and their presence there, though we perceive it, does not depend on our perceiving it. God delights in what God has made; God longs for the world to be as God intends.

If such a link exists in any natural religious perception of the world, it is also there in the understanding of God which Christians have received. We speak of creation and also of fall; we rejoice that in Jesus Christ God's reign has come, yet we pray constantly that it may come. We respond with praise and with penitence, with thanksgiving and with petition to God. Because of our longing, our delight is not an insensitive exultation that disregards the existence of suffering and wickedness; because of our delight, our awareness of the world's incompleteness turns into longing rather than immovable gloom.

This book is concerned with what is implied by the fact that the Church is the community whose delight in what God is known to have brought about in the world is joined to its deep longing that God's will might triumph over all that is ranged against it. In fact that Church is itself the fruit, the first fruit of God's longing, the instrument by which that longing is expressed in its prayer and in its action.

This book is also concerned with the kind of community the Church is called to be, in the light of the fact that it is placed in the world to express the longing of God. If that is so, the Church has to have a different way of being a community from that which we see in other human communities. It will be our concern to show that in a number of its present controversies, particularly, the Church is in great danger of forgetting that essential point about the manner of its existence in the world.

Human communities—all human communities—define themselves by the boundaries they draw (that is what 'define' means), by knowing who does not belong, and being aware of what is distinct from themselves. The word 'family' makes no sense unless it makes clear that there are those who do not belong. Name what group you like, and you will in the naming be calling attention to what is not part of it. All groups do it: the clubs, the communities we know, the ethnic groupings we belong to, all of them presuppose people who do not belong, and in the process draw attention to them. In describing the identity of any group we belong to we have an ironic interest in making sure that those who do not belong stay 'out there', and thereby contribute to our own sense that we are together 'in here'.

So we achieve a sense of belonging generally at someone else's expense. In the process of becoming members of something we create at the same time a multitude of others against whom, in some sense, we shall need to defend our interests. The loyalties and solidarities human beings make for themselves bring out some of their best qualities; at the same time, they engender some of the fiercest conflicts.

'It shall not be so among you' was Jesus' comment to the Church following his graphic description of the way which authority is exercised among the nations (Luke 22.24–7). The same comment might be applied to the way in which the nations define themselves and, by contrast, the way in which the community of the Church is to be constituted. The form of belonging which is appropriate to the Church is in radical contrast to the form of belonging we regard as natural in the ordinary groupings to which we are accustomed.

The reason for that contrast lies deep in the longing of God for the entire created order to be transformed into the harmony and beauty for which it was made. God's actions and desires therefore point in the direction of inclusion, of a special concern for the 'outcast', those who are beyond the boundaries created by persons and societies. What are excluded are only those things which themselves result in holding back God's concern to include.

The Church is the first fruit of God's longing. Its life together, therefore, does not depend on excluding people and groups, but on a witness to the constantly inclusive activity of a God whose concern extends even to a sparrow that falls to the ground. When that is forgotten, as it inevitably and frequently is, the Church becomes absorbed in various kinds of defence mechanism. In the process it loses its hold on that fundamental witness for which it exists, its witness to the longing of God. In the processes of exclusion in which it then engages, the Church ends up removing from itself the very sources of grace and hope from which it draws its life. 'Those who would save their life will lose it' (Matt. 10.39) is an observable and accurate description of the Church when it fears for its identity to the point that it seeks to secure it by means which are contrary to its essential purpose. Equally observable in that situation is the way in which the love of Christ appears among the excluded.

Why should this need to be said? Similar things have been said often enough: that the Church is concerned for the outsider and exists for those who are not its members; or that it is excessively turned in on itself and is in danger of becoming a sect—these things are being repeated again and again. What is the purpose of stressing it here in this way, and of bringing together two ideas, longing and belonging, that have no etymological relationship nor much else apparently to draw them together?

Those involved closely with the life of any Christian denomination find themselves moving from debate to debate. It is a time of great polarization, and there seems to be a struggle on every front. Whichever side you are on, there is no question about the amount of

3

energy such debates consume. As it becomes known which side you can be expected to take, so the pile of literature from pressure groups mounts.

There are labels given to the respective sides in such debates: liberal, radical, conservative, moderate, extreme and so forth. Labelling of that kind is a device for making connections of a kind among the various issues being discussed. If you can decide in advance which side a 'conservative' or a 'liberal' is likely to take in a particular debate you can save yourself a great deal of the energy you would waste in sending circulars to the wrong people!

The stereotypes are quite often accurate in what they predict, though most of us are better at accepting the accuracy of the stereotypes we apply to others than of those applied to ourselves. It seems to us that we think out all questions from first principles, never reacting through mere prejudice as other people do!

Yet even if those labels have a certain value, the connections they make between one issue and another do not seem to me to be very profound. They tell us very little about what it is that underlies our convictions about this or that matter. There was after all a heavy irony in W. S. Gilbert's song, 'Every boy and every gal/That's born into the world alive/Is either a little Liberal/Or else a little Conservative', and if we recognize the inaccuracy of that kind of statement in matters of politics, we ought to be willing to do so in matters of faith also.

There are indeed connections to be made among the various matters that divide different groups within the Church. Those connections need a far deeper analysis than is offered by the use of the obvious labels. It will not do either to repeat, as often happens, the assertion that some in the Church take their stand on God's revealed truth in Scripture and tradition ('traditionalists') while others accept only the authority of their unaided reason and personal experience ('liberals' or 'progressives'). Apart from the difficulty of finding anybody who professes to hold the second position, that kind of analysis simply lumps all kinds of issues together, offering no help in sorting out particular questions about the form in which 'revealed truth' presents itself or how we are expected to respond to it.

The intention of this book is to seek a different kind of analysis, and to propose that issues of longing and belonging arise constantly within the life of the Church, and need to be faced again and again. The book unashamedly takes as the starting point for its quest some themes that can be found in the Scriptures about the nature and purpose of the Church. Any other starting point makes the Church a free-standing institution that can invent its own directions to suit its convenience from time to time.

We shall be concerned here with two particular motifs in the biblical material, and with seeing how they relate to some of the difficulties in which the Church finds itself. It would of course be possible to choose different motifs and thereby produce a different emphasis; that is inevitable, although the themes that will be used here are so pervasive as to belong to the very heart of the matter. The first of the motifs has already been referred to. It is the notion that there is a fundamental difference between the kind of community that the Church is and other kinds of communities to which human beings naturally or by their choice belong. Chapter three will be concerned with that. Using two contrasting terms we shall look at the fact that the Church is set up on the basis that it is an *ecclesial* and not an *ethnic* community. It is that fact that determines its approach to all the issues that arise, and particularly to the most contentious ones.

The second motif, to be looked at in Chapter four, is the important implication of what is said in the New Testament about how those who are members of the Church come to be so. The contrast here is between membership by birth, kinship and descent, on the one hand, and adoption on the other. What distinguishes these two ways of becoming a part of the community is the place where choice lies. If the Church is seen as a community whose members belong by virtue of some form of kinship, then it belongs to a God who is to some degree constrained by the origins, backgrounds and achievements of particular persons or groups. A Church whose members belong to it by adoption do so by the action of a God who is free and unconstrained.

When we come to look at particular examples of struggles within the Church, it will be clear that each of them has to do with these two basic motifs: the nature of the Church as community and the way into that community. To make such connections is not, in any sense, to offer the final, knock-down argument in favour of taking one position rather than another in any of the issues in dispute. Instead it is to make clear that matters in dispute, even if they appear to be peripheral, are often the way in which struggles about these two central features of the Church's existence present themselves.

The subject of race and class in the Church with which we shall begin, is the one most obviously connected with our main theme. From the beginning, the Church had to concern itself with the constant tendency of ethnicity to become a governing feature in its life. So when ethnic conflict affects its life today, it is not hard to hear echoes of that original struggle. It is not especially easy to own it as such when it appears not as flamboyant racial bigotry and fascist rhetoric but as a cool, well-argued defence of things as they are and of well-established social arrangements.

Later chapters will be devoted to exploring two less obvious illustrations of this theme. The current struggle within all churches to come to terms with the radical change that has occurred in our time in the relationship between women and men is yet another encounter with ethnicity. It has become quite clear that the male sex with its long experience of dominance, and consequent difficulty in relating to people on any other basis, behaves increasingly like a tribe. It has its own way of doing things and a well worked out series of rationalizations to support them. From within, those ways of doing things appear not simply as the way things have happened to turn out, but as the way they ought to be, an internal morality in which the strong, the good and even the holy have become one.

That will appear even more when we consider how far the morality that has been created around the dominant heterosexuality of the majority is a rationalization for another form of tribalism. The debate about homosexuality presents a third area where the Church is engaged in a struggle to maintain its integrity as an ecclesial community against the strong pressure to become an ethnic one.

This third example raises in an especially sharp way how far tribalism is written into the way in which the bible itself has been interpreted. Certain texts have been understood as settling the matter; but if the Church is driven by that interpretation to abandon its primary call to be an ecclesial community, we shall have to ask whether those texts are really God's last word. In seeking to understand God's purpose for the powerful and wayward sexual longings so deeply built into the flesh of men and women it will have to think deeply about how longing and belonging come together in the Body of Christ.

It is of the essence of our life in ethnic groupings of one sort and another that we come to see our identity as deriving from a shared past. The most common ethnic question is, surely, 'What is your ethnic origin?' For so many purposes it is our past that decides what is to become of us and how we are to be valued: where we have come from, what education we have received, what we have achieved. We must not underestimate the power of the ethnic in human affairs; people fester in camps, are turned away at interviews, suffer insult and injury, all because of where they come from.

What will decide whether the Church can make any valid contribution to the fulfilment of its task, and indeed whether it has any claim to future existence, is whether it can assert its ecclesial identity forcefully enough against the strong temptation—never more strong than it is now—to accept the role of providing ethnic security for those who belong to it. Society at large would be very happy for the Church to accept such a role, and so to find its own insecure ethnic identity given a religious validity.

Unfortunately, the present time finds the Church of England struggling with issues of ethnic identity in a very literal sense. In an event in the life of its General Synod we find our first example that shows up the conflict very clearly. If we examine it more closely we may discover what some of the issues are and what resources of faith we have for tackling them.

2

An Ethnic Church?

'This is not a matter of racism.' The advice came quickly following the vote. In February 1989, the Church of England, through its representatives in the General Synod, had to decide whether it would approve new arrangements designed to ensure that a larger number of members of minority ethnic groups were elected to membership and thereby able to participate in the government of the Church of England at the highest level. The decision was made. The necessary majorities needed for the new arrangements did not appear, and approval was refused (see the General Synod's *Report of Proceedings* vol.20.1, pp.40–4 and 404–26).

It was understandable that those who were friends of the proposal should urge its sponsors not to get too angry, or react in too hostile a manner in their disappointment. This might have been bad tactics especially while there was still a chance of bringing the proposal back, and having it passed, perhaps in a modified form. So the received wisdom was, 'This is not a matter of racism.'

What may (possibly) constitute good tactical advice, however, need not be the same as the truth. Certainly those opposed to the proposal were at great pains to say that they were not motivated by any lack of desire to have more black Synod members. Their disagreement was only with the method proposed for securing a larger membership from minority ethnic groups. They believed that it was the act of introducing ethnic monitoring and affirmative action into the Synod's electoral process that was racist and discriminatory. As one opponent robustly (and revealingly) said, 'Are we no longer members one of another? Has God given up making of one blood all nations of men and—I had better be inclusive—women?'

The proposal before the Synod, at the request of its Committee for Black Anglican Concerns, was to ensure that in the next Synod to be elected no fewer than twenty-four members should belong to minority ethnic groups. Such debates naturally raise all sorts of issues, constitutional, theological, political and personal. They can all appear and make it very hard to tell which in the end was decisive.

But in this case, what was at issue was very near the surface of many of the speeches.

All the speakers agreed that within the Church of God there should be no question of ethnic distinction. All should be treated as persons, without reference to the colour of their skin or their country of birth. Indeed, it was evident that the variety of people's ethnic origin was for some speakers too awful even to contemplate, let alone mention. The making of special provision for people of minority ethnic groups would be something to which, as one speaker averred, 'no black man (*sic*) I know—and I have lived among them for a large part of my life and know many—who is worth his salt' would wish to be party. So it seems that to make special provision for the election of black people is patronizing; to speak on their behalf is not.

We are thus invited to believe that membership in the Body of Christ does not so much include or transcend our ethnic and other differences as obliterate them. Our Christian membership is as discrete individuals, cut off from the cultural roots and social background which have made us what we are and which might constitute a significant part of what we have to offer to one another. All sorts of gifts can accompany us into the Church, but not those that come with our ethnic origin.

There is no need to dwell on the many inconsistencies which appear in this kind of thinking. In other areas of its life the Church does not shrink from attending to people as members of distinct groups. Archdeacons and legal officers, universities and cathedrals, all have special privileges of representation. Crucially, in the distinctions made in its constitution between those who are ordained and those who are not, the Church is frequently prepared to deal with people as members of groups. Much of the political activity that surrounds the government of the Church arises from the way in which people organize themselves into groups to pursue certain causes and support those who agree with them. Does this mean that they are not one in Christ?

There was, however, a much more serious inconsistency in such thinking, one that made the whole opposition to some affirmative action on behalf of minority ethnic groups basically dishonest. It was that there appeared to be no hesitation whatever about acting, knowingly or unknowingly, in the interests of the dominant ethnic grouping.

What surfaced in speech after speech was an amazing confidence in the way in which the Church of England has traditionally done things. There is nothing, we were told again and again, to prevent anybody from being elected to the Synod and playing their full part in the government of the Church. The practice of one-person-one-vote democracy was quite sufficient to enable anyone, regardless of their ethnic background, to participate. Making any other provision is both patronizing and unnecessary.

Nobody would deny that the system of democratic elections is for many situations the best if not the only safeguard of liberty and of the right to participate in decisions. It has been in general a bulwark against autocracy and against the tendency of the rich and the strong to have undue power and influence. It is therefore quite natural that Churches desiring to have a synodical form of government, one that gives real authority to the laity of the Church, should opt for some kind of electoral procedure.

Yet it is precisely the intention behind voting procedures that was overlooked in the rush to defend the received way of doing things. For if the purpose of democratic processes is to make sure that the views of all count equally, must not that aim take precedence over the particular procedure that has been devised to achieve it? If there is clear evidence that the aim is not being achieved by that method, then the method must be examined afresh. In this instance, the experience of Anglicans from minority ethnic groups was that their desire to participate in the Church's government was being frustrated, and the decision that was taken meant the continued frustration of that desire.

What was being defended, therefore, was not the aim of democratic processes but a particular way of doing things, and doing things our way is precisely what ethnicity is about. Ethnic belonging is about being and acting in certain ways that mark you out as one of us. It is a constant tendency of dominant ethnic groups to assume that ethnicity occurs only in minorities; Chinese, Indian, or Caribbean cooking is often described as 'ethnic', while fish and chips are not!

It is dominant ethnic groups who are always in a position to deny the ethnic component in their own behaviour while noticing it so clearly in others. As many of the speeches in the Synod debate showed, the very mention of ethnicity can cause the members of the majority group to react with indignant horror and with a vehement denial that such considerations ever enter their mind.

Such responses are not new in the Church of England, and they did not need the arrival of substantial numbers of other ethnic groups to bring them to the surface. Kenneth Leech begins his trenchant study of 'racism in the cities and churches of Britain', *Struggle in Babylon* (Sheldon Press 1988), with an account of his early perception of the Church of England as an alien middle-class presence in a working-class environment.

> My earliest consciousness of 'class', in fact, was connected with clothes, indoor lavatories, telephones and books. The poor children—of whom I was one—whose parents could not afford new clothes at Whitsun, had no part in the precessions. Anglican church life in particular was associated with respectable clothing.... My first memories of going into a vicarage were of a house which was so much bigger than anything I had ever seen, very much 'posher' than my own house, and of the presence of large numbers of books (pp.1, 2).

What Leech is saying here, and what has been said by countless working-class people, is something about the dominant ethnicity of the established Church of England way of being. He speaks of the experience of the Church being 'them' not 'us', of being an alien within it and of its way of life as having nothing to offer him. It is a significant place to begin a book about racism, for it points to the fact that the fundamental issue in racism is one which pervades the fabric of human life and appears in a particularly tempting and subtle form within the life of the Church.

What makes it so difficult a phenomenon to deal with in the life of the Church is the ease with which it can be denied. Most of the ways of being that we have learned as the ways in which we identify ourselves as 'us' we have also connected in our own minds with what is Christian. So we lose touch with the distinction between our sense of what are Christian priorities on the one hand and our various ethnic preconceptions on the other. This is particularly true of concepts such as 'democracy': we have heard for so long how the vote is the guarantee of participation, and we have seen so many places where the absence of elections gives free rein to oppression, that we find it hard to imagine that the right to vote might utterly fail to provide a real medium of participation.

Yet that is precisely what the debate about special provision for the representation of ethnic minorities throws into sharp relief. The vote gives power to the majority; if the majority is in fact an ethnic group engaged in the defence of its own way of doing things, though refusing to notice it, it will never be possible for those who are not part of 'us' to gain admission. Dominant groups do not find their own ethnicity easy to recognize, let alone change.

In a chapter concerned with the fact of ethnic behaviour in the life of the Church, it is nevertheless important to point out that similar questions need to be asked about the failure of democratic institutions to make provision for the needs of other very deprived sections of society. We are increasingly in a position where the vote, which was the device for preventing those with military or economic power from oppressing the majority is now the means whereby a relatively well-off majority puts out of its mind the increasing poverty of minorities.

To return to our main concern, however, Leech is right to point out that the class captivity of the Church of England is a clear example of the same phenomenon, and many others involved in inner-city ministry have tried to make the same point. The uphill struggle to enable working-class people to exercise leadership within the Church, play a part in its government, and be accepted for its ministry, bears witness to the difficulty of identifying and acknowledging the power of class.

The debates are very similar to the one about provision for ethnic minorities: people will deny that class is a reality any longer; people will have stories ready of working-class people they have known who make a splendid contribution to the work of a parochial church council; and it will not be long before somebody who reads the Kenneth Leech quotation above will want to make the point that 'surely clergy need to read books.' Individually the points may have weight; but what they amount to together, and what needs addressing, is a determination to keep things the way we do them, to hold on to what makes 'us' who we are and keeps 'them' from causing things to change.

This book will attempt to show that this fundamental problem surfaces in relation to a number of current debates within the Church's life. Yet the selection of this first example, of the recent debate about minority ethnic group membership of the Synod, is not arbitrary. The point of starting here is that the concept of ethnicity is the biblical starting point for a consideration of God's dealing with us and God's call to the Church to come out from its various ethnicities and become the *ecclesia* of God.

In other words, kinship and affinity are the human realities out of which we are called, and our ethnic origin is the first and most obvious example of the power which kinship and affinity have over us. The fact of skin colour has made ethnic minorities obvious and immediate targets for the defensive, discriminatory activities of dominant ethnic majorities.

Class may indeed be just as powerful an arena in which the power of kinship and affinity can be asserted; so, we shall assert in later chapters, are gender and sexuality. But ethnicity is, both in contemporary experience and in the biblical record, the key that unlocks God's principal issue with the Church first and with the world thereafter; that issue is about the power we allow our kinships and affinities to play in our lives, and the way in which we use them to dominate and exclude. What is frequently said is that this matter is a secondary question of social concern, to be considered when basic matters of faith have been resolved. However the struggle against the power of kinship has been and is near to the heart of belief: what is at stake is our acceptance of the freedom of God.

That freedom finds its expression in a refusal to treat as final any particular way in which obedience to God comes to be expressed in any generation or situation. The distinction between the constant call to obey and the particular ways in which that call comes to be heeded is what constantly eludes us; and because it eludes us we are drawn into the successive manifestations of racism.

The history of collusion with racism on the part of Christians is one of repeated (and frequently deliberate) confusion between what are assumed to be aspects of 'Christian civilization' and what are simply the customs and practices of dominant or majority groups. That confusion, together with the possibility of distinguishing different ethnic groups by their physical characteristics, has led to the long and sad history of cultural, and often literal, genocide.

To bring mention of genocide into a discussion about a constitutional debate in the General Synod of the Church of England may seem first exaggerated, and secondly offensive to those who saw themselves only as having reservations about a particular electoral procedure. The advice to those who were disappointed at the outcome of the debate was indeed that they should avoid describing it in those terms. Yet without attributing active racial hatred to individuals, it is still important to draw attention to the processes which were at work in producing the situation which the General Synod was seeking to address and which its decision did nothing to remedy. The history behind the debate was the history of a terrible forgetting, a forgetting repeated in the outcome of the debate.

The act of forgetting, as it has appeared historically and as it reappeared in the result of that debate, is of two kinds. First is forgetting the humanity of those ethnic groups who may then be treated as at best subordinate and at worst subhuman. It worked itself out most clearly in the story of slavery, the reduction of whole nations to commodities to be traded. Whatever individual stories of kindness may be told, the physical cruelty and cultural and moral degradation wrought against whole peoples can only have been possible by a deliberate forgetting of their human status.

The second forgetting, the one with which this book is principally concerned, is the forgetting by the majority or dominant group of its own history of exclusion. It seems that we have an almost unlimited capacity for expunging from our folk memory, and even from our personal memories, those experiences to which the prophets were seeking to draw attention when they exhorted their people, 'Remember that you were slaves in Egypt.' The experience of exclusion, of having your humanity forgotten, is so much a part of the corporate and personal experience of most people that our eagerness to forget it is a massive tragedy.

To say that it is a tragedy is not to say that it is an accident. When Martin Luther King addressed the crowd at the end of the Selma to Montgomery march in 1965, he sought to remind the segregationists that their forebears had been taught the doctrine of racial superiority by those in power so that they would be able to maintain their own position. Those who forget their own experience of exclusion are all too likely to inflict such a sense on others.

So it is evidently very easy for those discussing other people's right to take part in the making of decisions to forget that the right to participate in the government of the Church could not always be taken for granted. It was only brought into being by devising arrangements which in their time also appeared as strange new developments, not at all in tune with the way 'we' do things.

In the ethnic behaviour of dominant and majority groups there is this double forgetting: there is the forgetting of the humanity of those who are pushed to the margins, and there is the forgetting of the experiences of exclusion and marginalization in the dominant group. Yet memory is not all that is suppressed in a refusal to change processes that exclude others from participation. When we consent to situations that keep others down we are suppressing not just memory but also hope.

What is tested by any proposal for change is not just our energy and imagination, our flexibility and ingenuity, but above all our desire. Are we still in touch with that discontent with the way things are and with our longing for the future God desires? What will enable us to accept the demands of any particular moment when those demands seem inconvenient or disruptive is the strength of our desire for a different future.

It was not enough, in the case we are considering, that there should be a belief in the equality of all ethnic groups before God and in the equal value of the gifts they bring. What was going to be needed were changes in the practices and cherished ways of thinking of the majority; and for that, the longing was simply insufficient.

The desire for a more inclusive Synod came most powerfully from the minority ethnic groups' representatives, who sensed their communities to be excluded. Their exclusion had resulted, as more than one speaker remarked, in the effective loss of a whole generation to the Church of England. But that desire encountered only a cerebral acceptance of the objective, and not a sufficient willingness to enact the means for achieving it. At the root of that desire and, also, of the lack of willingness to meet it, lies the basic issue of what full membership of the Church is and how it comes about.

If the Church is not an ethnic organization concerned to defend its ways of doing things as though they were tribal customs, that is so because it understands its members to belong by adoption and grace and not by right of birth. That means that the oft-repeated concern that those elected to the Synod need to be clear that they had achieved election by the generally accepted processes has to be put in question. A Church that exists by the free act of God cannot be surprised if at various times in its life it has to be prepared for developments that are not orderly and predictable.

This constitutional debate turns out, then, to be part of a continuing struggle for the Church to order its life according to the longing of God, the longing which brought it into being in the first place. Yet it is that very longing which the Church forgets when it overrides the needs of those who long, and whom God longs, to be included. At such times the Church simply gives a higher priority to maintaining itself.

That priority characterizes an affinity group, one that has its ways of doing things which end up by holding the community together. As we shall see, it is the reliance upon God's free graciousness that would produce a more open attitude to new possibilities and opportunities even if they can seem at times highly dangerous to the very character of the Church. At such times the argument is wrongly drawn by those opposed to change: the debate is moved on to the ground of loyalty to the Church's tradition.

As we shall see in later chapters, that is often how issues are debated in the Church: one side is said to be committed to an unchanging revelation drawn from scripture and tradition with an authority for all time; the other to have given primary authority to current ways of thinking, guided by the spirit of the age rather than by fundamental Christian truth.

Two things need to be said about this all too frequent misrepresentation of the situation. The first is that we seem to be living at a time when traditionalists are in many ways in the ascendancy. Perhaps then it behoves those who so describe themselves to ask whether they might be the ones becoming too attracted by the spirit of the age.

But the second point is the more important. It is that many of the debates facing the Church at the present time in fact drive us to look in a fresh way at the very roots of the Church's life and teaching. Those roots, so often said to be being forsaken in the rush to be modern, are exactly where we find located that powerful theme of the longing of God for a realm into which all are invited, bringing with them all that is contained in our diverse ethnic inheritances.

As we shall see, the Church has been made the child of that longing. It owes its life not to successions created by human authorities—natural birth and kinship—but to a divine choice—adoption and grace—which the ordered life of the Church is there to sustain and validate. So the task at this point in the argument is not to produce yet further examples of struggles within the contemporary life of the Church, but to return to the central scriptural themes to which reference has already been made. In that radical attentiveness to the originating period of the Church's life we shall find resources for addressing the issues of our time.

3

A New People

There is nothing unrealistic in the Scriptures about the problem of tribalism.[1] Whatever may be there about God's demands on God's own people, that was not because of any lack of interest in, let alone awareness of, the existence of other nations. The existence of those other nations was puzzling. They had different gods, different customs and different languages. At times the other nations proved more successful politically and militarily than God's own people, and that constituted a major religious problem for a people which believed itself to be God's special love, the chosen bearer of God's name.

The ancient tales which make up the first eleven chapters of Genesis can be seen as a statement of the framework of reality in which human beings live. There the issue of nationality is tackled in the story of the building of the tower of Babel. The story presumes that there was a time when human beings were all of one language. With a sense of their fragility, and with a fear of being dispersed over all the world, these primaeval people set about two enterprises: they decided to build a city whose top would reach heaven; and they sought to make a name for themselves as a protection against the dispersal and division which they feared.

God comes to visit the city and tower which the mortals are building, and concludes that if this enterprise succeeds there would be no limits to human achievement in the future. The method by which God defends the divine realm, and thereby establishes the boundary of human endeavour, is to bring about precisely the division which these representative human beings most feared.

So the Lord dispersed them from there all over the earth, and they left off building the city. That is why it is called Babel, because the Lord there made a babble of the language of all the world; from that place the Lord scattered them all over the face of the earth. (Genesis 11.8–9)

[1] For the contrast between *ecclesia* and *ethne* I am indebted to an unpublished paper by Harvey H. Guthrie Jr delivered at the Trinity Institute, New York, on 22 April 1975, at a conference on the ordination of women.

As this story presents the matter, nationality is clearly both virtue and vice. It is not part of what was there in that good beginning of which we read earlier in Genesis. In that sense it differs from either the creation of the animal realm consisting of many different species or the creation of humankind as male and female; unlike those instances of specialization, the diversity of nations is not one of the things God looked at and found very good.

On the other hand, the fact of nationality constitutes a necessary restraint on the overweening self-confidence of human beings and their refusal to accept the limitations placed upon them for the sake of their wellbeing. So nationality is also a divine creation, only in this case brought into being not because of its intrinsic goodness but because the nature of human beings requires that kind of restraint.

So those Jews who first heard the story of Pentecost would have been in no doubt that it amounted to a story of God transcending the boundaries established in the aftermath of Babel. It could not, however, be a reversal: the effect of Pentecost was not the restoration of the situation as it was before the Babel episode; what is brought into being is not the 'one language' of the primaeval story. What happens is that the gospel becomes accessible within and despite the boundaries and constraints which the diversity of human culture and nationality establish.

> Why, they are all Galileans, are they not, these people who are speaking?
> How is it then that we hear them, each of us in our own native language?
> Parthians, Medes, Elamites; inhabitants of Mesopotamia, of Judaea and
> Cappadocia, of Pontus and Asia, of Phrygia and Pamphylia, of Egypt and
> the districts of Libya around Cyrene; visitors from Rome, both Jews and
> proselytes, Cretans and Arabs, we hear them telling in our own tongues
> the great things God has done. (Acts 2.7–11)

The list emphasizes the point: the power of tribalism has been drawn, and God's address to humankind is not in any way to be obstructed by it. Ethnicity, the diversity of people's origins, remains a fact within the community of faith but it has no determining influence on members' standing either before God or before the community. Established for the purpose of preventing unrestrained human ambition, ethnicity can have no capacity to prevent the free and unrestrained activity of God.

The immense struggle which it took to accept this perception is in no way concealed in the New Testament. Specific issues within the life of the Church constantly raised the question of ethnicity. Which were the facts about people that belonged to their ethnicity: their history, culture, kinship, status and, indeed, their religion and morality? The life of the Church was to be built on the freedom of God to act irrespective of such matters. Which were the matters that belonged to the work of the Holy Spirit, addressing and converting people: the faith, hope, love and obedience that belonged to the heart of the gospel itself? On those there could be no compromise.

It was the struggle about what was ethnic about people, that which belonged to their origins and kinships, and what it was that belonged to their fundamental Christian identity that generated the strongest passion and produced the most creative theological insights in the life of the earliest Christians. The insight it created was one to which the Church has had occasion to return again and again at points of crisis in its history. For what has repeatedly been at stake was the freedom of God and, in consequence, the right understanding of what determined a person's standing before God.

So Paul draws a contrast between faith and the works of the law as a way of explaining to his Jewish readers which are the aspects of their obedience that belong to the demands and gifts of the gospel, and which are those that derive from their ethnicity. It is not on the grounds of Abraham's having been circumcised, his Jewishness, that they can claim him as their ancestor, but because of his faith, shown in the way in which he accepted God's promise:

> The promise was made on the grounds of faith, in order that it might be a matter of sheer grace, and that it might be valid for all Abraham's posterity, not only for those who hold by the law, but for those also who have the faith of Abraham. For he is the father of us all, as Scripture says: 'I have appointed you to be the father of many nations.' (Rom. 4.6–17)

Thus Abraham, the universal figure of faith, embraces as his descendants every conceivable ethnicity. The power of tribal consciousness to determine a person's standing before God, and that means in the first instance within the Church, has been overcome. Indeed, they are Abraham's descendants not in spite of their particular background, but precisely with that background as part of who they are; he is 'father of many nations'.

This view of the struggle with tribal consciousness is Paul's particular and passionate concern; it is also a theme that runs through most other strands in the New Testament. As Luke records the opening of Jesus' preaching in the synagogue at Nazareth, a clear marker is laid down that God's actions are not constrained by ethnic origin:

> There were many widows in Israel, you may be sure, in Elijah's time . . .; yet it was to none of those that Elijah was sent, but to a widow at Sarepta in the territory of Sidon. Again, in the time of the prophet Elisha there were many lepers in Israel, and not one of them was healed, but only Naaman the Syrian. (Luke 4.25–7)

Not surprisingly, the reaction was violent.

Conversely, membership of the succession of Israel is no guarantee that faith will be present or that the promise of God will be received. The Gospel of Luke opens with the account of Zechariah, who was not merely a Jew but at that moment carrying out his priestly duties in the Temple, responding with disbelief to the angel's promise of the birth of a son, and losing his power of speech as a result (Luke 1.5–22). The point is summed up in Jesus' blunt statement at the end of the account of the healing of the centurion's servant at Capernaum, recorded in both Matthew and Luke: 'I tell you, nowhere, even in Israel, have I seen faith like this' (Matt. 8.10; Luke 7.9).

How Christians were to live out that primacy of faith was the matter which the Council of Jerusalem sought to settle:

> It is the decision of Holy Spirit, and our decision, to lay no further burden upon you [non-Jews], beyond these essentials: you are to abstain from meat that has been offered to idols, from blood, from anything that has been strangled, and from fornication. If you keep yourselves free from these things you will be doing right. (Acts 15.28–9)

The fact that there are differences among the manuscripts concerning the demands listed in that resolution indicates just how strongly the debate continued. Which were aspects of Jewish Christians' ethnic inheritance and which were part of the true response of faith, to be hoped for from all who were presented with the gospel of Jesus Christ irrespective of their background, was certainly not resolved at one Council.

In the Gospel of John, Nicodemus, a Jewish elder, has it made abundantly clear to him that in relation to membership of God's realm there is a more basic requirement than having the correct background. 'In truth, in very truth I tell you, unless one has been born over again one cannot enter God's realm' (John 3.3). The problem about human descent is that it can never make sure of response to the spirit of God, because that response is characterized by freedom:

> Flesh can give birth only to flesh; it is spirit that gives birth to spirit. You must not be astonished, then, when I tell you that you must be born over again. The wind blows where it wills; you hear the sound of it, but you do not know where it comes from, or where it is going. So with everyone who is born from spirit. (John 3.6–8)

There is no reason to regard this struggle against exalting ethnicity to a decisive position as a novelty in the New Testament, invented by Christians out of their disappointment at the failure of Jews to respond to Jesus as the Christ. Certainly the earliest Christians did not think for one moment that they were inventing some new principle. In their minds they were simply conforming to a pattern amply laid down in the Scriptures, as the abundance of their quotation from the Old Testament testifies.

It is in any case clear that they had not received a set of scriptures that purported to describe the activities and demands of a tribal deity, a god at the disposal of a particular nation. It is true that in the early centuries the Israelites held in common with their neighbours in the Ancient Near East the belief that all nations had their own gods, guardians of people and territory. But it emerged very quickly out of their shared memory of release from slavery that the God of Israel was different; that their God was not able to be manipulated, and always demanded full obedience and trust. Furthermore, in the nature of their God's demands there were irreconcilable differences with other gods, and in the end their God came to be known as unique and universal. Such a God cannot be the private or guaranteed possession of a particular ethnic group.

As a result the Israelites were constantly called back by the prophets to an awareness of the demands which their allegiance to God placed upon them. With that recall went a constantly repeated warning against any simplistic reliance on a guarantee that they were God's own people. At the heart of that recall and that warning was the same conviction that informed the early Church in its struggle against ethnicity: that the world was in the hands of a God who acted towards it with complete freedom and out of a love that was not constrained by any cultural or ethnic limitations.

21

There can therefore be no escape, for Israelite, for Jew or for Christian, from the need to discriminate between the demands of a free and loving God on the one hand and even the very best features of our particular tribal inheritances on the other. The Epistle to the Galatians is the foremost example of a wrestling with that question, but as has already been said the struggle is scarcely anywhere absent from what we have received from our earliest Christian forebears. The gospel is to set believers free from what turn out to be purely cultural demands:

> I, Paul, say to you that if you receive circumcision Christ will do you no good at all. Once again, you can take it from me that everyone who receives circumcision is under obligation to keep the entire law. When you seek to be justified by the way of law, your relation to Christ is completely severed: you have fallen out of the domain of God's grace. For to us, our hope of attaining that righteousness which we eagerly await is the work of the Spirit through faith. If we are in union with Christ Jesus neither circumcision counts nor the want of it; the only thing that counts is faith active in love. (Gal. 5.2–6)

Yet the demand of faith has to be honoured:

> . . . do not turn your freedom into licence for your lower nature, but be servants of one another in love. For the whole law can be summed up in a single commandment: 'Love your neighbour as yourself.' (Gal. 5.13–14)

Yet this discrimination, an unvoidable task for the Church, cannot by definition be achieved by the use of some rule of thumb that will list clear and indisputable characteristics of ethnic obligations and the response of faith. If there were such a rule that would provide an infallible guide, it would either be so general as simply to beg the question, or specific enough to become, at another time or place, an inherited piece of ethnicity. God would have become, in our perception, bound by those rules, and the freedom of God would have been sacrificed. For specific commitments, demands and requirements that at one time express the action of a free and loving God towards God's creatures become inevitably at another time the inherited perceptions of a particular group or culture.

Yet the absence of some infallible rule does not mean there is no more to be said. We are not left simply exchanging opinions when difficulties have to be resolved. In the process of those initial, and crucial, struggles our forebears were taught some critical lessons about that act of discrimination, lessons which are recorded for us.

In particular they discovered in the experience of Jesus Christ himself the most difficult example of what that discrimination might involve. What they found was that he had chosen to become the one who failed to meet the demands of ethnicity, to become the reject of the community of faith, as the only way of being the agent of God's free activity.

> Christ bought us freedom from the curse of the law by becoming for our sake an accursed thing; for Scripture says, 'A curse is on everyone who is hanged on a gibbet.' And the purpose of it all was that the blessing of Abraham should in Jesus Christ be extended to the nations, so that we might receive the promised Spirit through faith. (Gal. 3.13–14)

It is for that reason that the Scriptures have consistently required their readers to accord a particular status to the situations of those on the edge of the community. They are those who may be the bearers of a message or an insight that shows up the point where faithfulness has become ethnicity. They are able to show up that point precisely because they have found themselves excluded. The parable of the judgment in Matthew 25 describes a Christ who has been found to be outside the community of faith, among the naked, the imprisoned and the sick: 'Anything you did not do for one of these, however humble, you did not do for me' (Matt. 25.40).

Those judged unrighteous demonstrate by their failure the inevitable failure of ethnicity itself. Human groups and communities cannot avoid creating a boundary around themselves and seeking their identity at the expense of those who are not members. The integrity and way of life of the community are often at stake; and we know of no way of preserving it other than by defending its boundaries, at whatever cost.

As that process occurs, it is even possible to be persuaded that the resulting exclusion of some is for their benefit: is it not for the good of the world that the integrity of the Church is preserved and the boundaries that secure its way of life are defended? And yet at the very point when that happens a barrier has also been erected against the freedom of God to act, to love, and to save as God alone chooses. It was for that freedom that the first Christians found themselves struggling, at the cost of painful debate and dissension among themselves.

It should be clear by now that any thinking about the Church and its life has to take seriously the powerful forces that are released by the way human beings seek to belong. Almost any significant development in our common life will raise the question: Is this still the Church, the Church to which I belong? If it changes, will I be cast adrift, cut off from the only source of life the Church can rightfully claim, the grace of God? Such are the inevitable fears of those within the community of faith when, as in those earliest days, the boundaries of the community are challenged and seem not to hold.

Because the fear of ceasing to belong to the Church in which we believe is so strong, the chance of ever admitting that any part of that commitment has become largely ethnic is small. It is only at the point when we make a serious attempt to go alongside those who have no stake in belonging because they have not had the right to belong anyway, that we have the possibility of knowing what the freedom of God might mean.

> Our altar is one from which the priests of the sacred tent have no right to eat. As you know, those animals whose blood is brought as a sin-offering by the high priest are burned outside the camp, and therefore Jesus also suffered outside the gate, to consecrate the people by his own blood. Let us then go to him outside the camp, bearing the stigma that he bore. (Heb. 13.10–13)

Expressed in the language of Jewish religion, these verses declare with the greatest force the dangers of ethnicity as a means of belonging. Those nearest the heart of a community whose faith has become an excluding culture cannot participate in God's free activity. That was possible for Jesus only when he went to the outside, to the place of curse, and that is where the Church is asked to join him. Only from that place is it possible to see clearly what are the marks of faith and what are the pieces of ethnic inheritance. The true possibilities of belonging are not seen by those who are protecting their own right to belong, but only from the place of those from whom belonging has not been a possibility.

We must now turn to see what pattern of belonging is appropriate to a community that desires to live under the free grace of God. What is certain is that none of the specific issues that cause major division within the Church can be addressed without taking into account the intensity of its members' desire to belong to that which is authentically the Church. That is the source of the passion with which they will be bound to resist anything that seems to threaten it.

What is also certain, however, is that such a desire and resistance are not new, any more than the challenges that arise from time to time to test them. There has been no time when there could be an escape from the challenge of a free and unrestrained God to views and practices which may have been a witness to faith at one time, and yet at another may have become the exclusive and excluding pattern of an ethnic group. There is no place or time which can expect to be secure from that central challenge; permanent belonging is, for the believer, always somewhere ahead. As the writer of the Epistle to the Hebrews explains as justification for seeking Christ outside the camp: 'Here we have no permanent home, but we are seekers after the city which is to come' (Heb. 13.14).

4

Children of Promise

When it comes to family life as we understand it, the Scriptures offer little explicit help. Given the priority the family holds for many people now, it is a great embarrassment that Scripture offers so little advice and so few models. Indeed the absence of models is more of a problem than the lack of advice. Patterns of life in families are more assumed than spoken about. Curiously, but undeniably, many of the key moments in the biblical story involve breaking with, rather than comforming to, expected patterns of kinship.

The inheritance rights of the eldest son are hardly a very common feature of our experience, except in the conservative institutions of royalty and aristocracy. That makes it easy to forget that the biblical world was one in which those rights are assumed. So the writer of the Epistle to the Hebrews can describe the Church as the 'church of the firstborn' (Heb. 12.23) and communicate an immediate sense of the special favour of God in a way that such an expression does not do today.

Yet in such a world we find again and again that God is not bound by those rules. Israel, God's chosen people, are not the descendants of Abraham's eldest son; Esau sells his birthright and the holy nation is born from his deceiving younger brother. It is the youngest of the sons of Jesse, David, who becomes Israel's great king, and Solomon his successor was in fact the child born to him by Bathsheba, the relationship that involved David in adultery and murder.

So we find that at key moments the normal rights of the eldest son do not form the significant links in the chain of divine action as might have been expected; but that is just the beginning of the way in which the ordinary rules of familial descent fail to be the means whereby the divine blessing continues down the generations. It turns out that the divine blessing frequently bypasses such ties of blood altogether. The supreme instance of the very ambivalent role played by physical descent in the biblical story is of course the tables of descent given for Jesus himself in the Gospels of Matthew and Luke. Both have genealogies that connect Joseph with the patriarchs of old; but both also make quite clear that they do not work to establish a physical connection between Jesus and Joseph (Matt. 1.16, Luke 3.23).

What is said in this way of Jesus himself is said about his followers also, who become that not through their physical descent but through God's unconstrained action:

> To all who did receive him, to those who have yielded him their allegiance, he gave the right to become children of God, not born of any human stock, or by the fleshly desire of a human father, but the offspring of God himself. (John 1.12–13)

It is not therefore surprising to find that the process by which people become members of the People of God is stated in terms not of birth but of adoption. Adoption confers all the privileges that go with being a naturally-born son, and in the case of Israel that is what God conferred on them. The contrast between natural birth and adoption is felt most keenly by Paul as he faces the rejection of Christ by Christ's own people:

> My sorrow is so great, my mental anguish so endless, I would willingly be condemned and be cut off from Christ if I could help my brothers of Israel, my own flesh and blood. They were adopted as sons, they were given the glory and the covenants; the Law and the ritual were drawn up for them, and the promises were made to them. They are descended from the patriarchs and from their blood came Christ. (Rom. 9.2–5 JB)

Paul goes on to insist, despite the pain he feels about it, that it is the promise of God that confers membership in God's people and not physical descent. This is not to speak of a God who is unjust, but to insist that membership of God's people is a matter always of God's free mercy, bestowed as God chooses. That is the only way of speaking of members of Christ's body:

> For all who are moved by the Spirit of God are sons of God. The Spirit you have received is not a spirit of slavery leading you back into a life of fear, but a Spirit of adoption, enabling us to cry 'Abba! Father!' In that cry the Spirit of God joins with our spirit in testifying that we are God's children; and if children then heirs. We are God's heirs and Christ's fellow-heirs, if we share his sufferings now in order to share his splendour hereafter. (Rom. 8.14–17 JB)

The purpose of Christ's coming was that the adoption should be conferred on the members of the Church (Gal. 4.5); such was God's intention from the foundation of the world:

> In Christ he chose us before the world was founded, to be dedicated, to be without blemish in his sight, to be full of love; and he destined us — such was his will and pleasure — to be adopted through Jesus Christ, in order that the glory of his gracious gift, so graciously bestowed on us in his Beloved, might redound to his praise. (Eph. 1.4–6)

There are only some half a dozen texts in the New Testament in which the language of adoption is explicitly used, and nearly all of them have been quoted. But it would be a great mistake to suppose that adoption is some peripheral metaphor, included by chance, and not necessarily to be given too much weight in considering the character of the early Christian community.

The truth is that this use of language is one of a number of ways in which we are confronted with the radical and painful nature of the New Testament Church's experience of God and of what it was to be a follower of Jesus. It is not too strong to describe that experience as one of arbitrary unfairness and an unnatural rejection of those entitled to love. There are other ways in which it is described; but the pain is not hidden. Despite it, our forebears were clear that only in God's free mercy, hard as it might be to receive, lay the world's salvation.

So accustomed are we to the idea that we should feel comforted by Christ's comment that there is more joy in heaven over one penitent sinner than over ninety-nine righteous persons (Luke 15.7), that we easily cease to feel it as an abrasive, and at one level outrageous, policy. In a sentence it cuts at any sense that there might be virtue in faithfulness and that such virtue might meet with a response of divine delight. To hear those words and identify oneself too quickly as one of the beneficiaries, as one of the penitent, is to miss the deep struggle into which Christ pitched his hearers.

Yet again, that aspect of Christ's teaching and ministry cannot be dismissed as resting on a text or two; it runs as a constant theme through what he says and does, and it is not hard to imagine the disturbed reaction which it encountered. What are people expected to make of a vineyard owner who pays one-hour workers the same as he agreed with those who worked there all day? How would a father expect his elder son to respond to the great feast arranged in honour of the return of his wastrel brother?

This note of arbitrariness and of the overturning of the natural order of things is struck not merely by Jesus' teaching but also by his actions. His relationship to the unclean, to the outcast, to those who for whatever reason had forfeited their status, or never had any, represented a constant enactment of the theme. Nothing is offered by way of additional benefit or reward to the righteous of the time, and meanwhile his meals are with publicans and sinners.

For the most part Jesus' teaching and action is among his own people, and they are his chief concern. But it is beyond doubt that the first Christians' perception of themselves as God's adopted children, saved by a free and generous God, has its roots in the logic of Christ's own ministry. The reactions of the righteous are too close to the reactions of Jewish Christians to the admission of non-Jews into the life of the Church to be a mere coincidence, let alone a distortion of Christ's ministry by his followers. We are dealing with an unexpected and unmerited mercy in both cases; in both cases there seem to be no benefits for those who might see themselves as expecting and meriting it; in both cases it is felt as arbitrary and unfair.

Yet the connection is at a deeper level still. What happens both in the ministry of Christ to those who have been judged unrighteous, and in the opening of the Church to the Gentiles, is the striking of a chord with the whole tradition of God's dealing with Israel. Paul's appeal to God's promise of a child to Abraham and Sarah is essentially an appeal to a moment that laid out the whole promise of God's dealing with the world. The promise was to a barren woman, and to a man in his old age; this was no ordinary and predictable birth, no merely 'natural' one; it was an event that declared God to be one who 'makes the dead live and summons things not yet in existence as if they already are' (Rom. 4.17).

Sarah's giving birth fulfilled a promise and at the same time it made one, the promise to call into being what was not yet, and in particular to summon into existence a new people. That people was to be constituted not in accordance with qualifications already in existence, but on the basis of the promise of a free and unmerited mercy.

So those who were not by birth members of the old Israel could be members of the new, because the basis of belonging was for all members that of adoption and not of flesh and blood. That was not a new departure, but had always been the case about the People of God. The opening of the Church to non-Jews was not just a carrying out of what could logically be derived from Jesus' teaching about and ministry to the poor; rather, his life and teaching *and* the admission of non-Jews to membership of the Church were both a living-out of the logic of God's promise to Abraham and Sarah, the moment which constituted the manner of God's dealing with his people for ever.

That promise opens out towards the future with an ever expanding vision of its meaning and implications. At the heart of the universe, as creator and sustainer of its life, is one who meets the deepest longing of all created beings with a promise that they will be loved and included in God's purpose for ever; and the 'for ever' means particularly at the points where they find themselves disinherited or excluded. If there is any condition attached to that promise it is that those who benefit from it should not speak and act as though with their own inclusion the process of inclusion had ceased.

It is always possible, and frequently happens, that those who have found themselves the inheritors of free and unmerited mercy then make themselves the arbiters of who may belong. At that point, to return to the discussion in the last chapter, the community of faith transforms itself into an ethnic one, defined by the criteria which are met, or not, by those who seek to belong. The character of the Church as the place where God's promise to Abraham is lived out disappears and its members find themselves part of an ethnic organization much like any other, with its own maintenance and the securing of the boundaries of its membership as its main objective.

In describing the character of the Church as a place of promise, the language of adoption has a vital place. Uniquely, it holds out to us the vision of a basis of membership for the Church that in principle knows no barriers and describes our own basis of belonging in terms which can apply to others. If adoption is the only means to membership of the Church, and it is, then the life of the Church cannot ever be organized on the basis of ethnic ties of either birth or achievement. And if adoption is therefore the common experience of all the Church's members, they have no basis for behaving towards one another, or towards those who are not yet members of the Church, as though there were qualifications of blood or merit which hold sway, or ought to hold sway, within it.

Yet it has to be said that to speak of adoption as the way of belonging within the Church creates difficulties for many. It seems in itself to express a conditional quality about God's care for people. It explicitly contradicts the notion that belonging within the Christian community is something which ought naturally to be the case, without further ado. It seems to strike a blow against the universality of God's love by making it dependent on a further act, that of adoption.

Such reservations have been given force by the whole history of discussions about baptism as the sign of adoption, and what happens, therefore, to those who die without being baptized. Those discussions, with their legacy of fear among those whose babies die without being baptized, have raised doubts about continuing to speak of adoption as the means of belonging to the community of faith. Do we not encourage another kind of ethnicity, elitism, by insisting that people are not by nature within the covenant of God, but only as the result of a further exercise of God's love towards them? Are we not thereby creating a category of God's unloved, or not yet loved?

To engage with this difficulty is to face the question: What kind of God is it whom we claim to know and what is the character of the love which is offered to us? Clearly if we wished to speak of a love for the creation in general, a holding in regard all of those whom God has made, it would then be intolerable to suggest that some might be excluded from that by a failure to undergo 'adoption' by whatever inner or outer experience that could be offered. Indeed, we could not by definition need 'adopting' into such a universal concept.

What is totally lacking from such a picture, however, is any sense that the love of God might of itself confer any special quality or status on its recipients. To be loved by definition, that is to be held in affection where everyone and everything else is too, is to lose what has been at the heart of the experience of the people of the Scriptures; and to be affirmed by one who affirms all things and all people in principle is hardly to be affirmed at all.

The experience of God described in the Scriptures is always the experience of being chosen, of being specially and particularly held. Yet it is precisely that sense of having been chosen that leads to the constructing of boundaries of birth and merit and to an excluding ethnicity, the very critical danger our language seeks to resist. How can we speak inclusively of God's dealings with us and at the same time acknowledge the experience of all those who have known that the love of God confers on them a very special standing?

There is hardly any more intractable problem in the attempts of human beings to form community than this one, and it is of course far from being exclusive to the Church. The need to preserve a sense of being special, without at the same time needing to be exclusive, rears its head in every family and group. Jealousies and sibling rivalries have to be taken for granted in all societies. Within the community of faith, however, the desire to be exclusive is easily given religious justification.

Yet at the heart of the process of adoption lie two things which have some capacity to keep our natural confusion between being loved in particular and being exclusive of others in check. At the heart of adoption lie both a longing and a promise: there is a child needing, we assume, to be somebody's child; and a prospective parent, someone with, for whatever reason, a space in their living and loving that has yet to be occupied. And out of that meeting of longings comes a promise that creates the relationship that previously did not exist. It is a relationship newly created, that does not depend on the sharing of a past, as blood ties do; for there is no shared past. It depends on the possibility and hope of a shared future.

Similarly, as has already been said, there is, in a religious view of the world, both a delight and a longing at the heart of our experience of the world. What is already is very good; what could be, what must be, what is intended to be—these arouse our deepest longing. The believer holds that such longing is not just a subjective experience but has its roots in the longing of God, that what is good might truly become as it is intended to be.

What believers have sensed in the heart of God, however, is not only longing. There is at the same time an assurance that what is longed for will also come to be; that is a sense of promise. This is not the same as imagining that all your wishes will come true. It is the conviction that the fundamental purpose of all things is being brought to pass, and that the longing for the fulfilment of God's purposes will not in the end be disappointed. Such a process cannot simply be left to itself; it involves the striving and longing, as well as the taking of initiatives and the suffering of disappointments. It requires more than the expected, the natural, the deserved; it needs also the unmerited, the surprising, the developments that surpass what is naturally possible.

The language of adoption captures something of that double experience: to delight in the good and to long for its fulfilment in the bringing to pass of God's good purposes; to have the sense of being part of a community that is special and being specially entrusted with the task of bringing that purpose to be, and yet to know that it would be the ultimate denial to allow that sense of the special to be protected by any exclusivity. In knowing that our membership of the community of faith is the result of a free and unmerited mercy, we are invited to share the hope that includes all within the possibility of that mercy. The remaining instance of adoption language in the New Testament holds both the delight and the hope together, and the exhilaration almost leaps out of the text:

> For I reckon that the sufferings we now endure bear no comparison with the splendour, as yet unrevealed, which is in store for us. For the created universe waits with eager expectation for God's sons to be revealed. It was made the victim of frustration, not by its own choice, but because of him who made it so; yet always there was hope, because the universe itself is to be freed from the shackles of mortality and enter upon the liberty and splendour of the children of God. Up to the present, we know, the whole created universe groans in all its parts as if in the pangs of childbirth. Not only so, but we, to whom the Spirit is given as firstfruits of the harvest to come, are groaning inwardly while we wait for God to adopt us and set our whole body free. (Rom. 8.18–23 NEB, *translation slightly amended*)

To know what the language of the Scriptures addresses and offers is not of course to be protected against the fears and insecurities that have given rise in every generation to a self-protecting exclusiveness in the Church's life. It does require us, however, to be more aware than we often are of the implications of being the Church and of making the kind of profession the Church's members make.

It is also worth taking further thought about the strands of resistance to the outsider we have noted in the New Testament, and the pressure to retain some hold on exclusiveness, which the Scriptures do not conceal. Both have their roots in the desperate quality of the need human beings have to belong, and the fierceness with which they will defend the possibilities of belonging that they have already gained.

Arguably, the issues of belonging, of community and of exclusiveness are the ones most dangerously unresolved in the human community in our time, and the ones about which the Church's own origins, history and experience could have the most to contribute. Yet it is equally clear that the Church is by and large very out of touch with the way in which the temptation to ethnicity has been faced in the past and the hard-won convictions that have emerged from that struggle. Because it fails to recall that, it also fails to make

33

the contribution to the human community which it could, and seems to have very little good news on that subject to share.

And for the community of people brought into being out of the experience of being adopted by the free grace and mercy of God, and for the Church that claims to be filled with the longing for all God's children to be revealed and to enter into their inheritance of freedom, that failure is a tragedy indeed.

5

The Male Tribe

Nowhere is the struggle for the Church's character being more passionately and tragically acted out than in the debate about whether to end the male monopoly over the orders of priest and bishop. While this struggle is engaging the whole Anglican Communion and shows every sign of spreading to Roman Catholics too, the principal place of engagement is currently the Church of England. So as legislation goes through its processes and groups organize to promote their position it is important to look closely at the nature of this struggle and what is basically at stake in it.

It is first of all clear that what is on the face of it a relatively simple issue is rapidly made more and more complex. As was the case in the matter of representing minority ethnic groups in the Synod, all kinds of arguments, central and peripheral, legal and theological, can be introduced into the discussion and make it more and more difficult to discern what is the heart of the matter—and that itself can be a matter of controversy.

The contention that we shall be exploring here is that the determination to preserve the offices of bishop and priest as exclusively male is yet another failure to grasp the nature of Christian membership. It is ethnic behaviour; it is a refusal to accept the ecclesial character of the Church in the way that previous chapters have described it, and a rejection of the nature of Christian membership as a free act of adoption by a generous God. It is the attempt, and it has ultimately to be a vain attempt, to reproduce in the Church a kith and kin identity which is the very thing that the Church exists to contradict. It is the male sex of the human species behaving as a tribe.

The signs that this is in fact the process into which the debate about the ordination of women has degenerated lie in both the political and legislative process and in the nature of the theological arguments being brought forward. Nobody, of course, states that they are in favour of a tribal Church; the arguments and the political processes as they appear all seem on the face of it to be about other matters.

But if in fact the totality of those arguments and those processes suggest an institution engaged in a prolonged piece of ethnic self-defence, that needs to be taken into account especially by those seeking to bring about an end to the male monopoly of the priesthood and the episcopate. Failure to do so can lead to an enormous waste of time and energy countering arguments that do not merit the attention they receive, and can amount to collusion with the tribal behaviour which lies at their root. Let us first look at the process of legislation.

The strategy in relation to the legislative process has been very clear from the first. Among the proponents the concern has been to have the best chance of success. So every opportunity has been taken to provide what are seen as 'safeguards' for those who will continue, even after the passage of the legislation, to be unwilling to accept women as priests (their ordination as bishops has not so far been placed on the agenda for legislation). The safeguards offered have been of two principal kinds: those for parishes, clergy and bishops who will wish to remain in the Church of England but be able to refuse the ministry of women; and those who will feel obliged to leave.

In the former case, there is a complex set of provisions for refusing to ordain, or to accept, women in priestly ministry. There is immense scope here for argument about detail: who shall have which rights, the length of time that the safeguards will operate, and so forth. There are almost limitless opportunities for thinking of groups and situations that need to be taken into account.

In the latter case, the provisions take the form of rights to compensation for those currently holding ministerial office and who will consider themselves obliged to resign if women are ordained. Here again, there are huge possibilities for the discussion, and indeed the creation, of detail and for haggling over what is to count as fair.

The strategy of the opponents of the ordination of women has been equally clear: it is to encourage, and in fact demand, such provisions as have been offered and campaign for them to be enhanced. Their evident ingenuity in thinking of affected groups and financial hardships and their zeal in campaigning for some reimbursement of what they describe as the 'cost of conscience' serve to prolong the process of formulating proposals and increase the energy devoted by supporters of the ordination of women to ensuring, as far as they can, that no stone is left unturned in the enterprise of meeting everyone's needs.

A further result, however, is a continual loss of clarity on the part of proponents of women's ordination about the principles that are at stake for them. For the opposition, this is not a problem: their opposition is fundamentally and in principle implacable; there are no modifications to the legislation, no amounts of compensation, no elaboration of safeguards that can in any way modify their objective which is the defeat of the proposal.

Such concessions therefore not only fail to mollify the opponents; they inevitably provide them with further grounds for attacking proposals which can be shown to be inconsistent or even unprincipled. Furthermore, the arguments over the legislation convey a message of their own: it is that to cease to bar women from the office of priest is to make a change in the Church's character so fundamental and revolutionary as to amount to a breach of some implied contract with the members and ministers of the Church. What else could be the justification for the language of safeguard and compensation? How delectable is the mess of pottage that must be prepared so as to induce priests to part with what they claim is their birthright of a lifetime's immunity from female colleagues?

The belief that ending the male monopoly of priesthood is a revolutionary threat to the character of the Church, is a belief held only by opponents; and yet it has been allowed to become the principle underlying the whole process. This is what is bound to happen in a tribal struggle. The way things have been is made the justification of how things are, and how things are is made into the yardstick of how things may be. The negotiations take place entirely on the ground prescribed by those opposed to change, and those who seek a different future allow themselves to be manoeuvred into a tacit, if not an explicit, acceptance that the beliefs of opponents are in fact the shared assumptions of us all.

We see further evidence of the tribal character of this dispute in the way it presents itself theologically, for as the legislation has been in preparation, so also the theological arguments about the proposal have been pursued. As well as the arguments offered on one side or the other by individuals and groups who are concerned, the House of Bishops of the General Synod has produced its own report setting out under various headings areas of agreement between supporters and opponents and also areas of disagreement (*The Ordination of Women to the Priesthood; a Second Report*, Church House Publishing, 1988). Our purpose here is not to assess all these arguments individually, or indeed to set out others: it is to look at this official document as illustrative of what happens when ethnicity becomes dominant in church life.

What we are presented with is a report which studiously avoids giving any indication of the relative weight of the various arguments presented, either in terms of numerical support within the House of Bishops or in its corporate judgment. That there is division is clear, and would have had to be owned in any report produced by the House of Bishops; but it is remarkable that in a body which is supposed to be the repository of the Church's primary teaching function the large majority known to be in favour of proceeding to ordain women did not insist on indicating their evaluation of the arguments presented.

The result is a report which, whatever words it contains, gives a very clear message to its readers: that the ordination of women raises the most enormous issues which are too deep for most people to fathom, and which produce even in the Church's appointed leaders both perplexity and division; that to act wrongly on the matter would threaten the most fundamental themes of Christian faith; and that the best that can be done is to show it as a very finely balanced judgment, about which the most prolonged study is necessary—even though on the evidence of the report itself it is unlikely to produce much progress.

Many arguments in favour of ordaining women are presented; but in so doing, the House of Bishops seems to be accepting the view of opponents that it is indeed a very dangerous and ill-advised disruption of the Church's life and work. Supporters argue in the report that the ordination of women is not a disruption of the Church's life and work but the removal of a vastly outdated impediment to it. But the shape of the document itself says the opposite.

In the same way, the report records that supporters believe that opening the order of priests to women is not an act of disloyalty to the gospel, but on the contrary the only way of making clear that the gospel is good news for women and men everywhere. Yet again, the Bishops' failure to decide among the arguments recorded says the opposite.

Thus tribalism captures the discussion. The governing assumptions are those presented by the way things are now and the main anxiety is to ensure that the past which has produced the present should not be overturned by the future. This becomes even clearer when the individual arguments presented for and against are examined. All of them turn out to be governed by attitudes as they have been formed in a Church where women are not ordained. The all-male priesthood that we have now not only has most of the power of decision but also, through its way of thinking, provides the ruling theological agenda.

The first area of difficulty for opponents of the ordination of women, and which therefore occupies the House of Bishops, is that of the priest as representative of Christ especially in the celebration of the Eucharist. The focus of the discussion is first whether the maleness of the incarnate Christ is to be regarded as a fact of significance, and secondly whether a woman could discharge that representative function.

There is much that could be said about this argument even on its own terms, and the view of priesthood which all who were party to the report say they agree with; there are signs in the argument that this exaltation of the celebrant as representative of Christ is rather reducing the function of the sacrament itself—let alone of the laity! What is far more serious, however, is the fact that the whole argument about representation is couched in terms that have to do with the satisfaction of the needs of the worshipping community itself.

So the very anti-ethnic quality of Jesus' own teaching about how he is represented simply goes unmentioned. Most strikingly those other representatives of Christ listed in the parable of the judgment find no place in this thinking.

> Then the King will say to those on his right hand, 'Come, O blessed of my Father, inherit the kingdom prepared for you from the foundation of the world; for I was hungry and you gave me food, I was thirsty and you gave me drink, I was a stranger and you welcomed me, I was naked and you clothed me, I was sick and you visited me, I was in prison and you came to me.' Then the righteous will answer him, 'Lord, when did we see thee hungry and feed thee, or thirsty and give thee drink? And when did we see thee a stranger and welcome thee, or naked and clothe thee? And when did we see thee sick or in prison and visit thee?' And the King will answer them, 'Truly I say to you, as you did it to one of the least of these my brethren, you did it to me.' (Matt. 25.34–40 RSV)

The fact that this material is not included in the discussion has doubtless to do with its not being the subject of disagreement, which is to say that it does not appear on the agenda of those opposed to the ordination of women. Yet in another sense what could be more relevant to the issue of Christian representation than Christ's injunction to look outside the 'tribe' of the recognized and esteemed to find him? What is certain is that the issue of representation cannot be sorted out by looking within the terminology and actions of a Church that conceives itself in so ethnic a manner.

This tribal captivity of the discussion continues as the House of Bishops considers the second area, that of 'headship and the exercise of authority', a bizarre and esoteric conversation. It seems that all that has been discovered in the secular world about women's contribution in positions of leadership in every area of life has either to be rejected as an offence against the created order or regarded as irrelevant to the ordering of the Church. A Church which so treats the discoveries and insights of the human community is truly opting for tribal separation.

Because this bit of the conversation has its shape and agenda prescribed so clearly by those for whom the ordination of women is a problem, it is noticeable that even the positive arguments are put with an air of apology and an absence of delight in the offering women have to make. It is thereby conceded by the elders of the tribe that women's place within it constitutes a rather grave problem set by God, but one which the men might be able with effort and ingenuity to resolve. That is what happens when you start from the perspective of those who are having the difficulty.

The ethnicity of the conversation continues as the House of Bishops considers the effect of the ordination of women on the unity of the Church. Again, the agenda is created by those who are anxious to prevent the ordination of women, as the eyes of the House of Bishops turn only to the Roman Catholic and Orthodox and then only to their official representatives.

The unity of which the report speaks is clearly the unity of the Church as presently constituted. The starting point is not the activity of Christ in 'drawing all people to himself'. That perspective would have required starting with a concern for those beyond the Church's own boundaries, and repenting of its separation from those who are profoundly alienated from its life because of the tribal attitudes symbolized by male exclusiveness in the ministry.

The same enclosed response appears in the chapter on the Church's sources of authority. At the start there appear to be possibilities of openness: 'Tradition is not an ever accumulating hoard of static material. It is living and dynamic' (p.149). But it does not take long for the agenda of those opposed to the ordination of women to move the argument into the question whether the 'tradition' of an all-male priesthood is for ever binding on the Church, and who would have authority to change it. Where now is that tradition which is not 'an ever accumulating hoard of static material'?

What we see here is the way in which the dynamic Scripture and dynamic tradition, with their constant theme of response to the new and to that which is outside and beyond our present grasp of reality becomes a selectively used system of tribal control. The result is to place those who are seeking to respond today in the position where they have to defend their loyalty to the Christian inheritance, while those who are neglecting some of that very tradition's most important themes can present themselves as its guardians.

Finally the House of Bishops considers the process of decision making on issues where the Church is divided. Does the Anglican Communion, let alone any single province of it, have the authority necessary for the making of a change such as this? It is made clear in any case that the question is academic for those who are opposed to ordaining women on theological grounds—if something is wrong in principle, nobody has 'authority' to do it.

There is also a profound unreality in the contention of opponents of the ordination of women that some higher authority is required for what is proposed. The report says:

> It is . . . inadmissible for a single Province of the Anglican Communion, or indeed the whole Anglican Communion, to take a decision on a matter which affects the unity of the Church and involves a change, or at least significant development, in the universal ministry. A decision ought, therefore to wait until it can be taken in the fellowship of all the Churches in a fully ecumenical Council. (p.102)

This cannot be a serious proposal of a means for reaching a decision about whether women may be ordained. It requires the summoning of a gathering of prelates some of whom are not in communion with each other, and who have shown no sign of willingness to convene such a gathering for any purpose whatever, let alone the settling of an issue in a Church whose ministry they do not in any case officially recognize. The postponement would be indefinite, in the hope, no doubt, that the issue would go away. As those bishops who are in favour say:

> Many of us, while acknowledging the integral relation between the ordination of women and the unity of the Church and the universal ministry, believe that a decision on the matter cannot be deferred to some indefinite future: it must be made, using faithfully the structures that do currently exist. (p.104)

And in words that should, if taken seriously, have rendered unnecessary many hours of unreal detail, they declare

> The failure of another Church to reform itself ought not to be a reason for the Church of England failing to act on the will of God as they perceive it. (p.104)

But however seriously these last words were meant, they could not be taken as decisive by the House of Bishops, trapped as it was in the agenda set out by those opposed to women's ordination. In a debate so fundamentally ethnic in character, it is the way things are that has to be seen to be the yardstick of the future, and those who claim to speak for the way things are who determine the shape of the conversation. Whatever is said by way of criticism of the arguments against women's ordination in the report, its shape is laid down by those who take the negative view, and it is therefore inevitably their message that is conveyed.

If the terms of the debate are as tribal as has been suggested, how is it going to be possible to break that pattern? How, to put it another way, is the theological initiative to be wrested from the guardians of an ethnic mentality? How does an *ecclesial* community, one that is whose members are called to contribute their ethnic backgrounds and gifts in the creation of a new people, respond to new situations, insights and knowledge in a way that is true to its nature? How does it first think about such matters (the theological question) and what, secondly, are the processes by which it considers change and executes its decisions (the legislative question)?

Ethnic communities think from the past. They ask how things have been and whether they need to change; if they do not, well and good. If they do, what they seek is the maximum continuity with the way things have been, and the change that is sought is the change of minimum adjustment. The Church is not an ethnic community; it is the first fruit of God's longing, and must think from God's future and ask how to prepare for it.

Ethnic communities also think from the inside outwards. Confronted with other communities, they ask what dangers they present, and what changes would be required for them to be accommodated. If they are to be accommodated, the question is what are the minimal changes that would make that accommodation possible. This is not because their members are grudging but because their thinking is ethnic: it assumes that its wellbeing lies in its own continuity, and that the heart of its life must be preserved as closely as possible to what it has been.

The Church, however is not an ethnic community: it is required to think inwards from the outside. It is required to assume always that the stranger may be an angel of God, bearing some new word or some new gift. It is to think this way not because its members are naturally more hospitable or less defensive than other people are, but because it has certain memories and certain longings: it is to remember that it is a community of those whose memory is of being a family constituted of outsiders, adopted in a great and continuing act of inclusion.

Its longing is to be part of that continuing inclusive action, one that turns no gift or word or person away unless they might themselves stand in the way of the inclusion of others of God's children. This longing is not some inherited personality trait among the members of the Church: it comes from knowing itself as existing only to prepare for God's ever more including realm, following one whose decision to accept death came also from the hope of what was set before him. It is that kind of remembering and that kind of longing which needs to shape the Church's thinking about an issue such as women's ordination.

The agenda of discussion would need first of all to be set by those wishing to cease excluding women from particular ministries. They would want to ask those who seek to resist the change questions such as:

Given that there are women who believe themselves to be called to priesthood, how will you justify to them refusing to consider their specific sense of call?

Given that any call comes from God, how can you manage to take the risk involved in denying that particular call without any evaluation? Have you read the numerous disasters which overtook God's people when new or unexpected vocations were ignored?

Given that our forebears were clear that the time for a hereditary priesthood was over, is it not strange for us to be retaining an all-male priest-hood when we know that sex is a hereditary characteristic?

Given that your membership in the Church is by God's free act of adoption, signified in baptism, how would you justify deciding the question of whether a person is called by an aspect of them as they were born?

What is the shape of the community of women and men that you long for, and for which the Church is a preparation? How would a Church that excluded women as women from certain aspects of its life be offering anything that might be called good news for women?

Nobody should consent to publish a report on the issue until these basic questions have been answered. Other questions, such as the effect on ecumenism or authority can only arise when the fundamental issues of Christian identity have been resolved. When a new issue is raised for the Church, as it is in this case, the first task is to test its relationship to those basic memories and hopes that constitute the Church. To begin with the questions that come from within the patterns of community life we currently have is to surrender to ethnic thinking and to fail to give primacy to the reign of God for which we long and in the service of which the Church exists.

If our being an adoptive community affects the way we are to think about an issue, it must certainly affect the way we make and implement decisions about it. An ethnic community is bound to start with the difficulties, with those who will be unable to accept change, with the pain that adjustment will cause to the existing community. An ecclesial community will begin with its call and with the truth it is now required to face. It will seek to reach a decision about that and only then work out what special provision needs to be made.

The ethnicity of our current processes lies in the fact that it is those currently excluded from priesthood who have to bear the cost of argument and delay for the sake of those currently within it. To become involved in bargaining about means of implementation before the primary principle is accepted and without any assurance that it ever will be is to sacrifice all claim to theological clarity. For the primary issue is that we should cease, now that the question has been raised, from patterns of tribal exclusion and receive the gifts that the Church is being offered. How we set about that is a secondary question that can only be dealt with once that primary decision has been made.

44

One further point needs to be added. As this book is being written the Church of England is already a long way into a process of thinking and legislating which, if what this chapter says is right, has been substantially influenced by the ethnic thinking of those opposed to the ordination of women. In accepting that kind of thinking many, including the majority of bishops, have been motivated by the desire to give the legislation the best chance of success, and the process thus far advanced must be taken to its conclusion in the hope that their judgment has been correct.

If it should end in failure, then those who believe the Church is called to stop its exclusion of women from priesthood will face a far more severe test than they have faced hitherto: does the adoptive character of the Church require us to find ways of answering the call we perceive, even at the cost of the order and discipline of the Church? The peril of going along with ethnic thinking is that it can lead one to suppose that such a sharp question will never arise. The truth is that such a question becomes unavoidable in a Church which fails to face up to its essential calling in the face of a pressing issue.

For the question whether women should not now be ordained does not as a matter of fact present itself as an interesting idea that happens to have occurred to a few people. Nor does it emerge from the personal ambitions of a few women who think they themselves should be ordained. It comes rather with the powerful energy of a generation that has recognized the patterns of behaviour that limit women's exercise of their gifts and is setting about dismantling them.

More than that: it comes with the passion of a Christian generation that has recognized its vocation as God's adopted children to cease from the ethnic patterns of male dominance, and honour the freedom of God to call whom God chooses. That powerful energy and Christian passion of our time come together as a great longing for the valuing of all God's daughters and sons, their insights and their gifts.

It is of course possible for that longing to be resisted and its logic denied. It is possible for a time to say to women who claim a sense of vocation to priesthood, 'We shall not inquire into this call or assess its meaning; we know it is an illusion because you are a woman.' It is possible, that is, to say to all women that there are perceptions they are not allowed to have and visions they are not allowed to entertain.

It is possible, for a time. But in a world where walls of concrete and divisions of armies have had eventually to give way before the sheer power of the longings of people, the Church cannot expect its resistance to that kind of longing to last for ever. And because it is with such longings that we are dealing, and because those longings have such clear roots within the life of the earliest Christians, the Church cannot expect its own authority and order to survive if it chooses to cling to the line of male ethnicity. How and when that longing will prevail may still be unclear; that it will is certain.

What has been asked for in this chapter is clarity about what is at stake in the debate about ordaining women as priests and bishops. That demand is particularly addressed to those who are supporters of change but who, as has been shown, are too readily drawn into patterns of thinking that govern the opposition. What needs to be held on to is the connection between the call for a priesthood inclusive of women and men and the most basic Christian conviction about a God who is free in both giving and calling. That freedom has been shown in the offering of membership in God's family to slave and free, male and female. The Church cannot for much longer resist that gift.

6
Love Unmentioned

The Church is not a tribe like other tribes. It is not a family bound together by a shared character or inheritance. It does not award membership as a prize for good behaviour, or as a reward for some attainment. Its existence is based on the free and generous action of God, whose adoption of us by grace is the only title we have to our Christian membership.

That has been the theme of this book so far. The Church is constituted in that way, it believes, not because it is an end in itself, some eccentric and arbitrary creation, but because the hope and destiny of humankind is to inhabit God's realm where such graciousness and generosity transcend natural and artificial divisions. To desire, to hope, to pray and to live for such a world is the task of the Church; and meanwhile it is charged with living out in its own life the future which it believes God holds out to every person.

We have looked so far at two examples of issues where this challenge to the church presents itself. In the case of the representation of minority ethnic groups in the General Synod of the Church of England, there seems to be no disagreement about the principle involved: all are agreed that the government of the Church requires the gifts of all groups and communities. What we discovered was a lack of willingness to take the action necessary to make that possible.

The last chapter, however, considered the question of the ordination of women as priests and bishops, where there is controversy about the principle itself. Those who seek to prevent that change maintain that the male monopoly of priesthood and episcopate is fundamental to what the Church exists to maintain. For others, that male monopoly is part of the tribal inheritance of the Church which the time has come to transcend.

So as we have seen, tribal reactions to new issues can lead to dissension and division. More menacing, however, are the occasions when almost complete unity can develop in response to what is seen as a threat from the outside. At that point, the adoptive character of our life within the Church passes, it seems, quite out of our minds, and we unite to repel what we see as elements that are not one of us, not our 'kith and kin'.

So it was when the Church of England's representatives came to consider the topic of sexual morality in November 1987.[1] In discussing the topic at that time the Synod was responding to a private member's motion condemning all forms of sexual immorality, but as its proposer made very clear in his speech, his concern was that the Church should express a definite mind on the subject of homosexuality.

Here was an occasion where the Church had to choose where its sympathies lay. Hostility to gay and lesbian people has increased, fuelled by the way in which the spread of AIDS has been linked to homosexual communities. Legislation has been introduced which prevents local authorities from 'promoting' homosexuality, and will also, no doubt, discourage many forms of assistance and counselling which local authorities have offered to those experiencing confusion about their sexuality. On the other hand there was strong evidence from within the Church's own membership, as represented in the Synod, of growing concern about gay clergy and their fitness to hold office in the Church. Who would carry weight in the mind of the Synod?

In the event there was not the slightest doubt. It became clear that the Bishops in the Synod had decided in advance that the most that could be done in the face of the rising tide of moral outrage was to support an amendment that blunted the sharp edges of the original motion. In terms of its demand for the exercise of firm discipline, the amendment was mainly concerned to protect the bishops' own prerogatives as the primary agents of the Church's discipline and pastoral oversight. To the gay clergy themselves, the principal objects of the motion's attack, it offered very little protection.

Their situation has been rendered extremely perilous by the November 1987 debate. A few speakers, including one or two bishops, complained about the tone of the proposition and its supporters' collusion with the gutter press; but there was no corporate dissociation of themselves by the Church's chief pastors from the stream

[1] See General Synod of the Church of England, *Report of Proceedings*, vol.18.3, pp.913–56. Further reflection on this debate appears in Jubilee Group, *Speaking Love's Name* (London, 1988); see also Rowan Williams *The Body's Grace* (LGCM, 1989).

of lurid tales of homosexual immorality which amounted to a public and general attack on a whole group of clergy who had in those circumstances no means of defending themselves.

The result could have been predicted. Honesty has been the first and immediate casualty; the pressure is there on all homosexual people to deceive themselves, and certainly not to reveal their self-knowledge to those whose task, in theory, is to care for them. All single clergy, whether homosexual in orientation or not, are vulnerable to rumour, gossip and suspicion, and nobody will ever know how many doomed marriages will be contracted in sad and wholly understandable flight from the risks of openness.

If such are the consequences for gay clergy, against whom the anger of the proposers of the sexual morality motion was principally directed, what is to be said about the implications of this episode for lesbian and gay people in general? Who can count the invisible multitude of the dismayed, those who thought that the gospel of Jesus Christ might have something to say to people who have found their own sexuality, for all its not having been chosen, something gracious and life-giving not just for themselves but for others?

The evidence of the Synod debate is that their experience is not worth listening to, that they are guilty by association with abusers and paedophiles, that they are not welcome if they are not celibate and likely to be suspected if they are. Among homosexual people no distinctions will be drawn, apparently, between kinds of behaviour as diverse as the exploitive, the loving, the committed and the flippant; all are pronounced guilty at the bar of the Church. For what you say about those within the Church's ministry has obvious implications for those on its fringes; and those to whom the Church seeks to reach out are not slow to hear them.

So what was said in the debate was both unjust to many within the Church's ministry and profoundly rejecting to homosexual people generally. We live in an aftermath characterized by dishonesty within and rejection without. This is the double note struck in a letter written to the Church press after the debate. It is regrettable that it was not printed at the time so that the support it offered in both directions could have been heard.

> I believe that [the debate's] outcome will confirm to that bit of 'the nation' with whom I work—children excluded from school for bad behaviour and other problems—that the Church has nothing to offer them. The

great majority of these young people come from broken homes where there has been little love or care; very few have ever witnessed stable and loving relationships with another person and consequently to be able to form a committed relationship with another person even for a period of six months represents a major breakthrough. In the case of a gay teenager this is doubly difficult. I think particularly of a former pupil who . . . having attempted suicide said to me afterwards, 'I wanted to tell you I was gay, but knowing you were in the Church, I didn't know what you'd think.' Despite most of the arguments I heard at the Synod I remain convinced that it is right to hope that this young man will be able to find a permanent, committed and loving relationship with another man.

Secondly, throughout the Synod's debate I was acutely aware of the pain of a number of gay clergy present. Not only did they have to listen to Tony Higton's catalogue of horror stories with which, because of their sexual orientation, they were by implication associated, but the best that even the tolerant voice of the Synod could offer them was 'compassion'. There was little or nothing I heard either to value these men as human beings or to affirm their ministry as priests. We could all tell stories about homosexual clergy, but I doubt that they would be of a kind cited in the debate or in the tabloid press. Rather, they would have to do with receiving sensitive pastoral care and wise spiritual counsel; of warm and generous hospitality and friendship which reaches out to welcome those ill at ease with many conventional Church gatherings, acting as a corrective to the view that the nuclear family is the be-all and end-all of community living; of those whose musical and other artistic gifts have enriched our experience of God in worship.

For those with eyes to see, the 'holiness of life required of Christian leaders' was apparent in the General Synod not in the crusading utterances of the instigators of the debate, but in the charity and restraint of those gay clergy present who, in the face of all the accusations and insinuations levelled against them, remained silent. (Jan Selby, unpublished letter, November 1987).

What is to be made of this episode in our Church's recent history? Many of us would look back on it as a nightmare were it not for the evident fact that its consequences are still with us in the signs of a dark age of intolerance. What emerged at the end of the debate was an overwhelming vote for a resolution affirming that marriage is the only proper context for sexual relationships, that 'homosexual genital acts' fall short of the Christian ideal and are, like adultery and other sexual activity outside marriage, to be met by a call to repentance and the exercise of compassion. Is this not simply the reiteration of a long-established, indeed unvarying, Christian tradition?

Yet to consider the resolution as though it were a simple restatement of traditional Christian values without taking seriously its context in the life of the nation and the Church is to ignore the effect of events on the way language is heard. We live in a time when homosexual people are under threat more than they have ever been since the Wolfenden report removed the criminal sanctions from homosexual activity between consenting adults. It had looked as though the centuries of discrimination culminating in the deaths of thousands of homosexual people in concentration camps might be coming to an end; but in our time they find themselves blamed for the spread of AIDS.

How can it be that at such a time the Church would think it right to administer to one of the most vulnerable sections of the community the full force of a moral rebuke, and accompanying threats of exclusion and discipline? Not surprisingly, given the character of many of the speeches, gay people diagnose those responsible for initiating the Synod debate as overcome by a deep fear of homosexuality. But that treats the instigators of the debate simply as so many individuals; it fails to notice the corporate and institutional nature of what took place, and which many of those who were present experienced. What occurred was predominantly a piece of tribal self-defence.

In the face of the evidence that traditionally accepted standards of sexual conduct are becoming harder and harder to communicate and more and more widely disregarded, the representatives of the Church turned on a group about whom they could readily agree. The experience of participation in the debate has been described to me as one of being progressively 'corralled' by the process of debate and amendment into the lobby in favour of a motion which it had been made impossible to oppose except at the cost of being represented as failing to support the Christian understanding of chastity. The fact that the debate and the resolution involved singling out for reproach a particularly defenceless group of people became a matter of entirely secondary importance.

No doubt many who participated in the debate, or voted for the resolution, would be affronted at the suggestion that they might have been participating in such a process of tribal self-defence. Their sense was only of defining and defending the Christian ethical stance

51

concerning sexual conduct in a society where that stance is being widely ignored with serious consequences; nobody will deny that there are important issues here, and that they include discovering an appropriate lifestyle for homosexual people, many of whom would wish to see such questions addressed.

That must not happen, however, by singling out for attack a particular group of people, in this case homosexual people, who then find their experience totally discounted. That is what constitutes tribal behaviour: to defend the boundary of the community on the basis of knowing in advance that some new experience cannot in principle be accommodated; to be sure, without needing to attend to actual experience, that the fruits of the Spirit cannot be manifest within certain personalities or relationships; and above all to believe that the integrity of the Church needs to be secured by declaring particular groups alien.

It has, of course, to be admitted that the issue of homosexuality presents a particular theological challenge, even compared with the other two examples that have been discussed. The unbroken tradition of interpreting certain biblical texts in a way that is hostile to homosexuality cannot be dismissed as irrelevant, and it is not being suggested that it should be. What is being put forward here is that there is a tradition, which is not only unbroken but also overriding, that asserts that the character of the Church can never be read off from the past in any exclusive way. Precisely because the Church is what it is, the community created by the free and unmerited action of God, the standing of a person within it cannot be determined by his or her conformity to some list of required attributes.

If, then, as is the case, the Church finds in existence a body who claim their same-sex relationships are neither illness nor problem but gift; if they declare out of their experience that such relationships are not barriers to their encounter with God but on the contrary have opened them to a greater depth of encounter with God and with one another; if they have come to see an unbending requirement of celibacy not as the setting free of their lives for openness to all, as it is when freely assumed, but rather as imprisoning; how then should the Church, the community whose members always belong to it by a gracious act of adoption, respond to such assertions?

Surely in the light of the Church's own history it has to accept that such new experience could in principle require it to reassess its own position; certainly it cannot simply disregard what it is told and incriminate by association those who are taking the risk of openness. To act in that way is simple tribalism. To be in any sort of position to think about a way of life appropriate for homosexual people the Church has to be open to hearing the story they have to tell and the insights they claim. To refuse to do so is itself to fly in the face of the Church's own Scripture.

For the ecclesial community, the community called out of ethnicity into the new people that has been gathered together by God's free act of adoption, new experience has always to be tested. What is being said is that lesbian and gay sexuality, so far from being corrupting and a danger to the lives of families, opens up its own possibilities of that faithfulness and commitment which are the characteristics of God's realm into which all are called.

The ethnic response, manifest in the General Synod debate, is simply to bring down barriers and assert that what we are being told is not so. The ecclesial response is to ask about the evidence, to listen with care and attention, and to search always for the possibility of a divine call to new perceptions that are inherent in any new experience. The truth will take time to emerge, and the Church's own tradition and experience contain substantial warnings against premature judgment. Above all, that tradition invites us to take special care before creating a new group of the excluded.

That is particularly important in view of some of the evidence that is already emerging. Those involved in caring for people who have AIDS or who are diagnosed as HIV-positive testify repeatedly to the quality of compassion and commitment shown by friends and lovers, and what is especially to be seen among homosexual people in those circumstances is borne out by the evidence of profound partnerships among gay and lesbian people elsewhere. There is doubtless more to learn and evaluate; but there are enough signs of the 'fruits of the Spirit' in such relationships to discourage the simple repetition of words of judgment.

In any case, the purpose of taking that example is not to come to a definite conclusion about it. It is to point to the real shortcomings in an ecclesiastical reaction that is hasty and defensive, and as such is not only untrue to the Church's fundamental character, but therefore unlikely to yield much in the way of discovery. Once tribal reactions take root, truth is the inevitable casualty, along with all those who have been subjected to a sense of rejection and condemnation.

Two further points need to be made: the first is that tribal defensiveness leads to a total loss of objectivity about what is being defended. The claim that it was marriage and the family that were being defended in the debate about seuxal morality lacks credibility in the face of the increasing—and alarming—evidence that within the Church no less than without there is much that is happening to marriage in practice that needs very careful re-examination. It would be important for those seeking to defend marriage against what are alleged to be the forces ranged against it, to promote a climate of honesty about what is actually happening to marriage in our time. In such a climate it is quite likely that the experience of homosexual people in living out commitment in a hostile environment might turn out to hold not a threat against marriage but promise for it.

The last point in the examination of this particular example is this: we hear again and again the attempt to characterize the debate as between those who respect the witness of Scripture and tradition and those who seek to revise it, between the defenders of the faith and its subverters, between 'liberals' and 'conservatives'. This way of seeing things adds far more heat than light to the debate. The fact is that this is far from being the first occasion in the Church's history when what was thought to be immutable came under challenge from new claims and new experience. Sometimes, but not always, that which was thought to be unchanging in the tradition turns out in fact to be so; but sometimes what was thought to be a defence of the truth turns out to be a mistake.

How shall we decide? Perhaps it will only be with difficulty and after much further struggle. But those who listened to the 1987 protagonists of an unbending attitude to any lesbian and gay lifestyles may detect in their stridency, in their lack of self-criticism, in their wilful refusal to admit into their minds any counter-evidence, grounds for believing that what we were seeing here was an ethnic rather than an ecclesial response to people and ideas we find difficult.

And if they do detect that—as I do—they will want to assert on the most traditional, biblical, basis that the Church was not made for that kind of response. It is here as a new people, bound together not in their conformity, even to ways of thinking that have been found good, but in their awareness of having been adopted freely and generously by a God whose loving graciousness constantly seeks out and reclaims what had been thought lost for ever. It is no service to marital faithfulness or to the security and love found within it to make of it a form of tribal kinship from which those who do not achieve it can be seen as outcast.

As with many things that have claimed the Church's attention down the generations, the question may turn out to be not so much what we have to say to homosexual people, but what it is through them that God might be saying to the Church.

7

The Elders of the Tribe

So the Church is not a tribe, but a new kind of people. It offers to humanity the possibility of membership in a new kind of community, open to new possibilities, relying for its existence on God's free and gracious act. Yet it often does not seem that way. It appears instead singularly anxious to protect its boundaries and guard itself against what might be new. In the process it imagines that it is being loyal to its fundamental character, but is in fact, as we have seen, forsaking it.

We have seen evidence of that in each of the three examples we have examined. When it comes to making it more possible for members of minority ethnic groups to play their full part in the leadership and government of the Church it is united in favour of the principle; in practice we are unwilling to make the necessary adjustments to our practice to enable this to happen.

On the question of the admission of women to the priesthood, there is no unity about the principle, and as a result it is the agenda of the opposition that dominates the discussion. What becomes all-important is to demonstrate that such a change would, or would not, change the received character of the Church as we have known it. The actual lived experience of women who have sensed a call, and who have in the eyes of their congregations demonstrated authentic gifts for that ministry, has to take second place to arguments about what has or has not been the case and what weight is to be attached to it.

In the last example, we found the representatives of the Church apparently united on a principle that is opposed to any recognition of experiences of faithfulness and commitment among homosexual people. Here the Synod united against a piece of experience that is judged by the tradition to be unacceptable, even if there is evidence of creativity and fulfilment in some same-sex relationships.

It does not seem particularly easy for the Church to live out that call to be a new people; instead the evidence is of negative responses and defensiveness. Yet that cannot be because there is disagreement in principle about what is said in Chapter 3 about the character of

56

the Church: the idea that the Church is a new people called out from among the nations and invited to transcend the natural barriers of race and class is hardly one that would be challenged in theory. Nobody is to be heard suggesting that the Church is to be an ethnic group alongside others.

Nor will there be any disagreement with what is said in Chapter 4 about the nature of Christian membership. Every celebration of baptism recalls the adoptive nature of our inclusion within the Christian community. Christians will not be found maintaining that their belonging is a form of kinship, let alone a reward for goodness or conformity. That our membership arises from the free action of a generous God is hardly a matter for debate.

Yet if that agreement is there in theory, how does it come about that on any specific issue the debate settles very quickly into being between those who see a threat to the boundary of the Church, which needs therefore to be defended, and those who see in some new experience or insight a gift from God? Is there perhaps more of a case for exclusiveness than has appeared up to now?

There are certainly important strands of exclusiveness in the biblical record. There is a determination that Israel shall not emulate the other nations. In the post-exilic period a concern to maintain Jewish religious observance leads to an exclusiveness of life that undoubtedly plays a crucial part in maintaining Jewish identity. Under successive occupations the people's strength of purpose seemed to demand the prohibition of any significant association with the people and customs of the surrounding civilizations.

The processes of exclusion are very evident too in parts of the New Testament. Certain groups are deemed to be a danger to the integrity of the Church; commands are issued to exclude them or avoid association with them. Very firm statements are made to the effect that the faithful are being misled and that the truth of the gospel is being compromised. The need to set up structures and make statements that safeguard the central message of the Church from dilution or subversion arises from the very beginning of the Church's existence.

To that must be added the long history of the discerning and removing of heresy and the practice of excommunication which have characterized the Church throughout its history. Could we ever expect there to be a Church that did not have to draw lines around itself at certain times and make decisions on certain issues that would result inevitably in the elimination of some of its members? And if we do, it is surely important to accept that there need to be criteria for the drawing of boundaries, and that those might look very like descriptions of a Church whose members have in some way to conform in order to belong.

Objectors to the ordination of women, as well as those opposed to any form of acceptance of homosexual relationships, certainly believe that we are at such a time. In taking that view they speak as part of a tendency to see the strength of the Church as lying in the drawing of firmer lines around its edges. This tendency is reflected, for example, in decisions about baptism policy, where firmer requirements on those presenting children for baptism are frequently proposed.

Clearly there has always to be the possibility that some person, or set of ideas, will be so frustrating to the purpose for which the Church exists that exclusion will be the only remedy if the integrity of the Church is to be safeguarded. It is possible for ideas to be so hostile to the Church's aim, and for practices to be so alien to its life, that the only way in which to protect it from corruption is to resort to exclusion. No church would possibly renounce that option completely.

Yet the risks involved in that option have to make it a last resort. A Church which claims to be following one who was so evidently the victim of exclusion has to take very careful thought before taking to exclusion itself. 'Outside the camp', where those excluded are to be found, is also the place of Christ. History presents too many examples of the exclusion of those who turned out later to have been right. Too many prophets have been rejected, if not actually killed, for the truth for the Church to take lightly to the path of rejection itself. It is not in the harshness of its boundaries that the strength of the Church lies, but in its willingness to seek and be alongside those who are outside it.

It is natural enough for those who are committed to the Church's life to see their role as gatekeepers of the truth, protecting it from corruption, from wolves in sheep's clothing, from thieves and robbers, from all, in short, who seem to correspond to the biblical images of danger to the gospel. Deep in the psychology of religious belief itself lies the quest for certainty and clarity which can easily turn into an arrogant or a punitive disposition.

Our concern, however, is not so much with the disposition of individuals as with what happens when institutions see their role as defending truth, a role which is frequently felt to justify the sorts of response which we have called 'tribal'. In many institutions such responses are defensible in that they accord with the purposes for which those instituions exist. But what are we to say about the tendency to tribal response when it occurs in a body which exists on the basis of a mandate to a different, non-tribal, form of corporate life, offering a non-tribal future for humankind?

One of the most obvious places where the effect of the pressure towards tribalism can be seen is on those whose task is to exercise leadership. In the chapter concerned with the ordination of women I referred to the way in which the report of the House of Bishops on the issue shows strong signs of having been diverted into accepting the agenda of those opposed to the change; in the chapter concerned with the debate about sexual morality, I referred to the way in which the bishops, faced with what they saw as the certainty that a motion hostile to homosexual practice would be sure to be carried, bent their minds to securing some softening of the tone and implications of the resolution. Do these responses reflect something of the demands and pressures on leadership when tribal responses are rife?

In the process of learning the work of a bishop over the five years prior to the writing of this book, I have found nothing more spiritually demanding than that particular pressure. It has generated a whole vocabulary about unity and collegiality, full of much that is beautiful and true, and yet all of it fraught with the greatest imaginable danger to Christian truth. At the centre of that vocabulary lies an insight about the nature of the Church as committed to a shared following of Christ and a shared understanding of the faith. Constantly threatening that centre with the danger of corrupting it are the less exalted realities of tribal self-protection, and the particular burdens that places on the elders of the tribe.

Among the most dangerously half-true understandings of the role of bishops is that they are to be the focus of unity in the Church. At the heart of that perception lies one of the most profoundly Christian of instincts, that we are called to bring together and not to divide, to seek and not to lose. The perception is a pastoral one, grounded in a vision of Christ as the one who broke down dividing walls and established peace. Strife and dissension can be a real wound in the heart of a pastor, inflicting a sense of failure as nothing else does. As a result, conflict becomes something to be avoided above all and healed as quickly as possible whenever it appears.

Yet the perceived call to a chief pastor to be the focus of unity is not only founded on the instincts of the pastoral person. If that were all, it would be easier than it turns out to be to bring about the recognition that it is far from always pastoral to avoid causing conflict; it is also evident that doing what the lost and alienated want is far from being always the best way to seek them. No pastor would on a moment's reflection deny that the most ultimately unifying thing to do is sometimes to bring about conflict, and almost always to face it when it does arise.

What adds to the power of the idea of the focus of unity is a whole doctrinal and liturgical inheritance. Doctrinal, because of the tradition that the bishops are a vital part of the Church's continuity in faith, and that not to be in communion with the bishop is not to be in communion with the Church. Liturgical, because the perceived role of the bishops in ordination and confirmation, visually enacted time and again in their visits to the congregations in their care, is to be the representative of the universal Church in its relationship to its local manifestations. Ruptures in those relationships do not only therefore invade bishops in their personal life as pastors; they appear to threaten the very role itself.

So the notion of being a focus of unity is not one to be dismissed as of no account. The centrality of reconciliation as a theme in Christian faith and history makes that impossible. However qualified, by talk of 'unity in diversity' for example, or by stressing the other marks of episcopal ministry as teacher and leader, the demand and the desire to focus unity for the Church is bound to be deeply rooted in the bishops' self-perception and therefore to affect the way their ministry is exercised.

Therein lies the danger. For the concept of the focus of unity is also capable of exploitation under the impulse of tribal self-defence. That exploitation need not come from others; all the potential for it is already present in the formation of bishops to be the focus of unity. The desire to unite quickly becomes the desire to stay together at all costs, and the wish to pursue a ministry of reconciliation degenerates, often unnoticed, into a fudging of issues and the extinguishing of dissent. That dissent, too, need not be the dissent of others; it can just as easily be the voice of uncertainty, doubt or opposition within themselves.

The matter is further complicated, and the dangers further enlarged, when it is not the individual bishop who is being considered but the bishops as a corporate body. What emerges in that context is the development of the notion of the bishop as focus of unity into the idea that the bishops have the responsibility of acting corporately as that focus. That appears most strikingly in the doctrine and practice of collegiality among bishops as the only way in which the unity of the whole Church can be safeguarded.

Here again we have a concept of immense spiritual significance and at the same time full of immense danger. It witnesses to the essential corporateness of the Christian enterprise and the fundamentally shared nature of Christian ministry. When, as is so in my case, you have spent nearly your whole ministry working as part of a team, and are now engaged actively in encouraging others to see ministry in that way, it is especially hard to be critical about collegiality as an idea.

Yet it is vital to be critical about it, and particularly about its capacity to serve what I have called an ethnic rather than an ecclesial identity for the Church. Colleagues are meant to consult with one another, not acting unilaterally in matters of importance. They are to hold to decisions and policies that they have arrived at with their colleagues and to which they have given their consent. They are to accept that when they speak and act they are bound, however unwittingly, to affect their colleagues, and in some sense to commit them by what they do and say. They are bound to offer support to one another in the challenges of ministry.

Yet such a notion can also endanger the possibility of dissent. In its emphasis on staying together and on loyalty, what does it have to say about issues and situations which are bound to drive people into separate and opposing positions? At such points it tends all too quickly to lead either to an oppressive demand for loyalty come what may, or an empty form of anonymous pluralism, of the 'some think this . . . some think that' variety, in which the struggle over the issue is simply given up.

The potential of collegiality for being corrupted by mere tribalism is very apparent in such situations. Two things happen; the first is that loyalty on the part of the dissenter is stressed to the exclusion of the equally vital matter of loyalty on the part of the body to the one who is driven in conscience to dissent. The loyalty thus becomes an ethnic and not an ecclesial idea; it is loyalty to the body as it already exists and to its perceptions as they have already emerged, to which obedience or at least outward conformity are required. It takes no account of the essential, ecclesial notion that truth may exist outside what is known or accepted now, that it may lie with the one outside the consensus, who may be the bearer of the authentic perception.

The other tribal development in the concept of loyalty is that it excludes the possibility of other, external and overriding loyalties. If bishops, as part of their calling, are to have a 'special care for the outcast and needy', what does that say in circumstances where the demands of the outcast and needy are in conflict with their colleagues' existing perceptions? What is the task of the focus of unity if that unity is ecclesial and not ethnic? If it is to embrace those who are isolated or even alienated by some existing consensus?

I continue to reflect on the exercise of my ministry in the light of my experience in the autumn of 1986 when I had to make the decision whether to be a communicant at a service where the celebrant was a woman priest ordained in Hong Kong. I read what I wrote then from a position very close to the experience, and the correspondence I received from those who found my action supportive, and I wonder why I found the matter so hard at the time, and continue to feel so strongly the pressure of tribal conformity. What are the resources that might sustain a positive openness of the kind that would be needed if the unity a bishop is to focus is to remain an ecclesial one, not reduced to a merely tribal conformity?

Before venturing to answer that question, it is important to observe the significance of this brief discussion of the tribal pressures as they appear to those in positions of leadership. For it is very easy for those on the fringes of the Church, and especially those who find it an exceedingly alien structure, to believe that its life and decisions are the result of giving far too much attention to the concerns of its hierarchy and far too little to those of its 'ordinary' membership. It would be understandable if they perceived a discussion of the problem bishops have in maintaining an ecclesial understanding of the Church as yet another attempt to divert the reader's attention away from those who are really experiencing the exclusions and rejections that a church caught in ethnicity imposes on its most defenceless members.

That is not my intention. There is no doubt that bishops, like other leaders, focus the reality of the challenges of the Christian life, both because that is what they seek to do and because that is what is demanded of them. The demand, and the expectation, that it should be unity they focus is what places both honesty and leadership at risk; but clearly their experiences, not least the challenge I have just discussed, show a great deal of the often hidden expectations of the Christian community as a whole.

That is why it is also instructive to see how one writer evaluated my reflections in 1986, focusing on the question of the resources a bishop might have for meeting this particular challenge. He took up the closing reflection I offered in a *Times* article on the event, when I wrote that:

> Bishops do focus the Church, but what they focus is the Church as it is. Being a focus of disunity is not therefore in itself a sign of pastoral failure.
> (*The Times* 11 October 1986)

Peter Walker, then Bishop of Ely, in his book *Rediscovering the Middle Way*, reflected, in words which move the whole discussion on to a different level:

> It surely is not a sign of failure, but on one condition: that the disunity which is focused in the bishop is held by him in a Godward reference. We here touch the mystery, but the central and to a degree the public mystery, of a bishop's prayers and that will have its bearing on the no less real question of his people's own vocation to prayer. (Mowbray 1988, p.110)

The introduction of prayer at this point in the argument is not in order to remove or conceal the dilemma, but to relate it to the other theme which has lain behind this book, that of the role of longing in belonging, and specifically the place of the Church as the firstfruits of the longing of God for a world that is new and whole. For the unity which the Church is required to make plain is not the unity it experiences as it exists now, but the unity which, like every other mark of God's own realm, exists ahead of us, to be prayed and striven for as that for which humanity most deeply longs. Not only humanity either: God also longs that we should face the truth of our divisions so that we can attain to the real unity God promises. By comparison with it many of the forms of unity we currently experience are at best flawed and at worst a pretence.

What always threatens to turn the unity that is focused by bishops and lived out in the Church into a mere ethnicity is the loss of the painful sense that the unity in which we are called to live is always in some sense ahead of us. At the point when unity is a matter of satisfaction rather than of desire, we face the threat that it will be a unity based on the kinship we have already discovered rather than on the adoptive and gracious act of God. It is the future and unrealized quality of what God holds out to us that is the crucial defence against our tendency to make of it something we have achieved, or must ourselves defend.

To examine the vocation to prayer of an ecclesial community is to be invited into one of the most difficult areas of human experience, that of unfulfilled desires and aspirations. At the centre of many of the issues mentioned so far is the question, what is to be said about those aspirations and desires that seem at the moment to be unfulfilled? What is to be said about the fact that many of them seem to threaten the unity we have and force us into division? How does the inclusive and costly unity into which the *ecclesia* of God is called out get established in the face of all the evidence that human aspirations are in conflict with each other and that meeting any of them is likely to prove divisive in the community?

It is that fact of human existence that forces us to consider the people's vocation to prayer. Would our belonging be closer and survive more readily the conflicts and debates we currently witness if our longing were deeper?

8

The Power of Longing

This book began not with the Church, whose debates and dissensions have occupied many of its pages, but with human dissatisfaction. It is natural to want things to be different, and there is an intimate relationship between delight and desire, between joy and longing. That connection comes, in the mind of the believer, from the very consitution of things, and has its origin in the character of the God who is the originator and sustainer of all that is.

Yet we find dissatisfaction extremely difficult to live with, and the mood of acceptance is easier for us to accommodate to religious belief than the mood of longing or desire. We do not find it at all easy to know how to respond to those whose aspirations will cause change and disturbance, and faith is more comfortable in the task of quenching desire than of stimulating it. Those who have desires that cannot be gratified without causing disruption to the world we know are seen as the cause of division and dissension; it is seldom the defenders of the way things are who are regarded as the source of any ensuing trouble.

Nor is it any coincidence that two out of the three examples that have concerned us are ones in which sexuality is involved; among all human desires that is the one whose power has been such as to unnerve communities of faith from time immemorial. Here more than in any other area religious belief has had the function of discipline and control. In theory all might accept that sexual desire is no more prone to derail a human life than other desires, that it is a gift from God and part of the goodness of creation. In practice, the response of religious believers is far more ambivalent.

So the celebration of the erotic has, with notable exceptions, not been a prominent feature of the life of the Church. Marriage has most frequently been seen as the means of disciplining that aspect of human life, giving to sexuality a more utilitarian function in procreation. So the relational side of marriage is grounded in 'the mutual society, help and comfort which the one ought to have of the other', not specifically connected to the sexual nature of the marriage bond. Where the connection is made in modern Anglican liturgy, it is again utilitarian.

> [Marriage] is given that with delight and tenderness they may know each other in love, and, through the joy of their bodily union, may strengthen the union of their hearts and lives. (*Alternative Service Book 1980*, p.288)

The hierarchy is clear: bodily relationships serve mental and spiritual relationships, and not the other way round.

So longings are on the whole seen as spiritual enemies, and as such need to be conquered. At the very least they are dangerous and need to be disciplined, and that is far more likely to be the instinctive reaction to them than that they might be seen as welcome. Sexual desire is only the most obvious instance; the desire for riches, for food, for drink, the various ambitions that are characteristic of human life, all are difficult to celebrate, and the religious mind turns far more readily to the need to keep them under control than to seeing them as a really good aspect of the created order. It seems that the only spiritually valuable desire is to be rid of desire.

Yet this can hardly be a valid way of regarding the various longings that are so intrinsic to our being. At least it has to be said that our bodily existence is intimately tied up with the fact that our bodies are endowed with the capacity to seek what they need, and that the most basic human desires are necessary to the survival of the individual and the species. There is no evidence to suggest that regarding desires as wrong has any effect in reducing their power; if anything the opposite is true. What happens if desire is condemned is that it goes its separate way, a realm declared to be without meaning in the life of faith.

In fact desire has played a far from negative role in the development of Christian belief. Conversion has very often followed on a strong sense of attraction and need, and the language of prayer and worship is full of passion.

> O God, you are my God:
> eagerly will I seek you.
> My soul thirsts for you; my flesh longs for you
> as a dry and thirsty land where no water is.
> So it was when I beheld you in the sanctuary
> and saw your power and your glory . . .
> My longing shall be satisfied as with marrow and fatness.
>
> (Ps. 63.2,3,6)

Such language of longing finds its echo throughout the Christian tradition, from the attractiveness which drew people to Christ to the passionate desire evident in the prayer of the mystics to experience the fulfilment of their desire for the fullest union with God.

All of this suggests that Christians might have just as much interest in kindling and nourishing desire as they evidently have in controlling or directing it. It is easy to gain publicity and engender vast quantities of shock and horror by speaking as though the major problem facing our Church and our society is the rampant and unchecked nature of evil desires wherever we look. Is apathy really the most desirable human condition? Is it even the best ground in which the seeds of the gospel can take root? Surely there are vast tracts of both society and Church where nothing at all of any consequence can be expected to happen unless the roots of desire are stimulated.

A sadly brief but very pertinent protest against the superficiality of much religious treatment of desire appeared in an editorial by Grace Jantzen in *Theology* in March 1989. She establishes first that desire is

> . . . one of our basic icons of the divine nature. According to the Genesis stories, when God shares God's being in creation the result is male and female with all the yearning which sexuality implies. Throughout Scripture, God is portrayed as a God of longing love, whose desire for the people of Israel is urgent, who is pained at their apostasy with the searing pain of a rejected lover, and who exults in their response with the exultation of reciprocated desire. As we get deeply in touch with our desires, even—perhaps especially—those desires which cannot be gratified, we get a poignant glimmer of the relentless intensity of God's desire for us.

Jantzen goes on to argue that perhaps the most important way to encourage spiritual growth would be to 'bear witness to the sheer beauty of God, the wonder of divine attractiveness. The greatest blasphemy is to make God dull.' Her protest is not an uncritical appreciation of all desire, far less a proposal that the best that can happen to desires is always to be gratified. On the contrary: Christians witness to the true desirability of Jesus, which arises from

> . . . the incredible beauty of his compassion, justice and freedom. In the broken body and the blood of Christ is all the beauty of God. To recognize and be drawn toward that glory in the face of Jesus Christ is therefore to increase in commitment to the oppressed and the marginalized, the ignorant and the sick.

67

The fear that often comes to the surface in the Church by talk of women as priests and of homosexual relationships is above all else the fear of desire. Like all groups that think about themselves as ethnic groups the control of desire becomes the most important way of safeguarding the integrity of the tribe. As our first example, the response to the desire of minority ethnic groups for representation in the government of the Church, showed all too clearly, the Church does behave frequently as an ethnic and not an ecclesial body: its struggles concerning the ordination of women and its view of homosexuality are all of a piece with that.

Yet it is desire and longing that have been the true forces for integrity within the life of the Church. They are what have kindled the aspiration of those who have been attracted to the following of Christ even when the Church in its inherited wisdom declared that they should not be or could not be. It has been so from the beginning that the creative—and attractive—forward movement of the gospel has been made possible by its constant and resurgent desirability to those whom the Church saw as outside its range.

If the Church remains unwilling to make the changes necessary to enable the participation of more representatives of minority ethnic groups in its government it betrays the limits of its own desire. It may want such participation to happen—but it certainly does not want it enough. It may desire that women play a fuller part in the Church's ministry, but it hopes that that desire can be held within bounds, the bounds of its own making. The Church hopes that its message will reach homosexual people, but has difficulty overcoming its own inherited revulsion enough to want to extend the gospel's embrace.

In being content with such limited desires of its own, the Church fails to assess adequately the desires of others, and that means not being sufficiently aware of the attractiveness of the things of Jesus Christ. To encounter the continuing desire of black people, after all that has happened to them, to remain within our Church and to participate in its life on the basis of so small a set of adjustments we are asked to make is indeed a humbling experience. Are they noticing something that we who have belonged for so long are missing?

Having consciously experienced for twenty-five years and more the ministry and sustinence of women seeking ordination and those making common cause with them, my strongest sense is of being amazed that after the succession of painful rejections and turgid debates they still offer themselves. Perhaps the Church would prefer it if they simply disappeared. But is it not vital to receive their presence as evidence not only of the power and persistence of their desire but also of the immense desirability of that which they continue to seek?

It is of course common to find among the arguments against allowing women to be ordained the suggestion that the case of those offering themselves for ordination is based on the 'mere feeling' of being called to that ministry—with the clear implication that the Church cannot base its decisions on mere feelings (is it the fact that they are women's feelings that makes them qualify as 'mere'?). That is right. But when such desires become widespread and have shown their persistence, it is just possible that they may witness to a desirability that those too long accustomed to having their vocations accepted are failing to notice.

To be in contact with lesbian and gay people asking for their experience of love to be given value by the Church is to be in contact with some very moving expressions of commitment. It is also to be made aware in a fresh way of what acceptance in the name of Jesus Christ can mean, and of how easy it is to take that meaning for granted if you have not had to struggle for that acceptance yourself and have ministered blessing to heterosexual relationships without having to ask such searching questions.

To state the obvious, what is desired is not necessarily desirable; some things that are desired may not be desirable yet or in the way they are desired. But the existence and persistence of desires to be part of the Church's life and witness and of its ministry are not to be dismissed either. They are evidence of an eternal, unfading attractiveness. They have been the most significant source of energy behind the Church's evangelistic enterprise for there is no greater encouragement than to rediscover the goodness of the good news through the eyes of those who respond to it. A perennial difficulty the Church has faced has been the response of those who in various ways are felt to be inappropriate, or whose responses have new things to teach us about our own response and about the gospel itself.

A moment's reflection on some of the implications of what has been said in the earlier chapters about the character of the Church should make this much less surprising. What is adoption, after all, but the meeting of the need of a child for a family and the overflow-ing of the desire of prospective parents for a child? And yet all are aware of the difficulties for the parents, for the 'natural' children of the family and for the adopted child that are inherent in that product of the meeting of desire with desire. There is the sense of arbitrar-iness, of the fragility of the old relationships and of the new, and the power of the feelings that are unleashed once the security of 'normal' family relationships is broken.

There is something very secure about the fixed order of things, when everything goes according to rule. Even the victim of that security, the person who ostensibly gains nothing from it and would gain most by change, can be found opting for safety rather than change. When the prodigal younger son receives the privileges of the firstborn there is a powerful reaction, and such has been the constant experience of the People of God; it is God's firstborn, always finding that God's blessing is, after all, bestowed elsewhere.

For the negative side of the safety of the established order of things is precisely its effect in quenching desire. The milk and honey of the land of promise had a remarkably deadening effect once the promise was fulfilled. It became enough—it became everything—to hold on to what had been gained. To do that almost required a forgetfulness of what it had been like in the days gone by to be one of those on the outside, for whom the established order of things had produced nothing and could offer nothing. For those who have forgotten what it is to be longing for what lies ahead and is better, all that matters is to hold on.

Such holding on is of the essence of ethnic living. It requires that you identify your kith and kin, those who will make common cause with you because they have what you have and stand to lose if you lose. Ecclesial living only makes sense when there is some desire for a new kind of future to be called into, one that you have not earned and could not possess, greater than now seems possible, not attainable by present skills or current plans. That can only be known by those who are still full of desire and longing; it is lost on those who are satisfied with what is if only they can keep it, or who have given up hope and therefore dare not long for what they know cannot be attained.

If we are seriously concerned, and the Church seems to be, about rampant and uncontrolled desire, the remedy is clear. It is not to endeavour to quench or control desire; it is to kindle desire for the attractiveness of the world God has in mind, so that people long for it and will live for it. Such desiring is the prayer to which the people of God are called. It is no remedy to engender contentment, because our desire is the one clue we have about what walking with God might be like while at the same time inhabiting the world as it is, and our discontent is the first source of energy taking us towards the reign of God.

Jesus declared blessedness to lie in being hungry now, in being thirsty now, in being mournful now. In such a condition the human person knows there is something missing, something to seek. By contrast those who are rich now, who are content now, who are comfortable now—they are declared to be in the woeful state of having had their reward. There is nothing for them to want or expect or pray for. The present is all, and the best that can be hoped for is that you will be able to hold on to it. What Jesus creates as a Church is a fellowship of those overcome by desire, whose vision is of the future God is making, and who pray 'May your reign come' because they know they need it to come.

Meanwhile there is membership by adoption and grace; it is a form of belonging that knows it cannot be grounded in what we have achieved or in that to which we are entitled, and for that reason it cannot be the kind of privilege that is defended by being held tight. It rests only on the promise of a future we might share in God. It can only be understood by those who know there is something better than the world we have seen and been offered, and who long for that world to be.

To write as an English Christian is to be aware that our nation has been offered, and has come to desire, a world that is the opposite of community by adoption and grace. We have been offered a world where participation is by achievement and competitive entry, and for over a decade seen our society irresistibly drawn to it. The Church's own life, as the three examples we have taken show only too clearly, has become a gigantic process of collusion with those who believe such a world is to be desired. We have joined in an exercise in holding on, in excluding those who might endanger our way of seeing things, and the privileges we have come to enjoy. In such a Church, in the midst of such a world, it is easy to stop seeing the essential attractiveness of those people and gifts we reject. There is nothing about them to be longed for; they are only a threat and a danger.

71

What is remarkable, and hopeful, is that in some way they, the excluded, have not lost their desire and their longing. They can still see that what they seek, acceptance in the fellowship of Jesus Christ, is irresistible, is still worth wanting, a promise that is meant for them too. Their persistence in their desire, or rather the persistence of the desire in them, is a miracle of grace that has much to teach us of what that calling to prayer is about. They know, whatever may be said by the councils of the Church, that the promise is for them, that they have been told that they are accepted in the fellowship of the beloved.

I would invite those who have voted against them in the councils of our Church, against their participation, against their gifts, against their attempts at loving, to receive what is said here not as blame, but as an invitation to look at their sisters and brothers again. Are they not surely part of us, and is our life together not the poorer by their exclusion? Is not their continuous, waiting presence a gift to be received? When we have looked again at them are we not bound to *want* them?

What is more, do they not cause us to lift our eyes towards those who are beyond them, those whose lives the world's injustice makes a misery but whose longing eyes are full of the attractiveness of God? Do not our present opportunities to say 'Yes' to those whom we currently refuse give some clue as to the expansive future that awaits us? It will be full of like opportunities to discover the attractiveness of God in those who have been counted as nothing, in a world where blessedness has come to reside in having rather than in desiring. The Good News will travel to the ends of the earth if only we can break the habit of holding on to it so tightly.

This has been an attempt to get to the roots of that habit, which lies, I believe, in tribal patterns of thinking which are contrary to the purpose of the Church. Those patterns of defensiveness lie at the heart of the issues that dominate our Church, not the claimed disagreement between 'liberal' and 'conservative' theologies. I have declared my belief in a Church that is an ecclesial, not an ethnic, community, a body to which we belong not by right of kinship but by a shared experience of the grace of adoption as God's children; if there are those who believe that the Church can be shown from its Scripture and its tradition to be other than that, let them say so, and we must argue it out. But I shall be astonished, for I believe that this understanding of the Church is only what the Church has itself always in principle professed.

In so claiming, I have focused on current issues of controversy closest to the Church in which I serve. Ultimately, it is to be hoped, the argument can move on to issues which, from a global perspective, must seem at least as pressing if not more so. But failure to tackle tribal thinking close at hand engenders habits which will and do paralyze us globally. In one sense what the Church of England decides is of minor significance; in another, tribal thinking in one place supports it everywhere, and it is for each of us to identify it where we can and undermine it as best we may.

Fundamental to that undermining is a desire that the Church should attend in a vigorous way to that aspect of its faith which lies ahead, which has to do with what we long for and what we believe God has promised. In all the argument about what the past has taught us, and about who is rightly holding on to it, we are threatened with the loss of something utterly central: those forebears of ours who first acknowledged Jesus as risen from among the dead believed that the new future they hoped for had dawned. Is it too much to ask that in any argument that develops we might insist on knowing what taking one position or another has to say about the *future* God has promised the world? To ask that question in any of the debates I have examined would be quite transforming.

This book is not, however, written only in longing; it is written also in the delight that is part of that longing. I write about the beauty, about the ministry, about the nourishment available to us from those whom we are even now excluding because I have known it. In knowing it I have found it converting. In the twenty-five years since I was allowed to hear Martin Luther King spell out his vision of a new people, not only hearing it but experiencing its beginning in the streets of Alabama, its attractiveness has remained clear to me.

One experience does not, however, last twenty-five years and the refreshment of it has come again and again in groups of people who despite all forms of rejection would not be diverted from their claim to be God's adopted daughters and sons. I know that my own image of Christ is drawn in large part from what they have shared and the graciousness with which they have done so.

They have also taught me much to delight in even in the Church that has rejected what they offer and in which I serve. Many are the gatherings I have known where through the distress involved in their presence has still appeared the fundamental desirability of the Christian Church—even when it professes with too much assurance that we are already God's new people. We are after all the bearers of God's promise, and the children of God's longing.

9
Belonging in God

I have pursued what has been in part a journey through the possible and actual perils of Christian membership. It has not been hard to see the sources of the defensiveness and the possessiveness which participation in the life of the Christian community can bring. It is not far from a deep-seated awareness of having been incorporated into the community of faith to a passionate clinging to the detail of the Church you know, and a fierce defensiveness in relation both to its boundaries and to its character. In all this it is the good that seems so worth preserving and the good that is so dangerous.

For in most of the attitudes and practices which this book has been concerned at various points to criticize there is a deep root of conviction and Christian experience. The energy that is put into becoming a participant in the government of the Church, into standing for election and into giving many hours of time to the work that is involved, is very close to the energy that with grim determination will seek to prevent any alteration of the electoral process to allow others to join in.

The sense of vocation that sustains people in ministry and draws out from them strength they did not know they had can also be turned into a strong resolve that what is seen as the basic framework of that ministry does not get altered. Equally evident is the road that leads from a zeal for righteousness in one's own life to a refusal to enter into the very different circumstances others face and to examine openly the possibilities which their varied personalities and capacities open up for them.

Writ large in the corporate life of an institution, such zeal and such convictions are what fuel the tribal styles of behaviour which this book has sought to name. Whatever view any reader may take about the particular issues and examples described here, nobody with any experience of a church can have failed to notice either in themselves or in the groups of which they are part these immensely strengthening and at the same time dangerous instincts.

At the centre of them are powerful longings, for closeness and intimacy, for security and nourishment, for life itself, which are basic

75

to human living. They are also basic ingredients of religious belief, contributing to its power and attractiveness. Religious people can manifest apathy no less than unbelievers can; but religious belief cannot in the end be apathetic; it taps into resources of human desiring which if not the basis of faith are closely connected with it.

Such longings, religious belief apart, are immensely powerful. Desires do not have to turn into prayers to achieve what they desire, and human wanting has brought about changes that might have seemed quite impossible. For the believer, however, they do turn into prayers, and that in turn opens up new sources of energy and possibility. For some of the negative features of tribalism that have been examined in this book come into being because of the certainty with which believers identify what they long for, and also pray for, with what they know: a life as it is and the Church as it is become not merely good but also answers to prayer. At that point, they become unquestionable, and all that threatens them with change becomes the enemy of God's own gift. So if tribalism is contrary to the Church's character, how are we to deal with tribalism in prayer?

It was a painful journey that our forebears had to take, and they had to take it often, away from the understanding of prayer which they received from the nations around them. For that understanding involved belief in deities whose responses to the desires of their nations was to validate them, giving to their rulers and their territories a foundation in the life of the gods in heaven; so absolute power was consecrated, wars were made holy, and the only morality was the preservation of the nation by whatever means the deities required.

Such gods are easier to pray to than One who questioned structures of power when they resulted in the demeaning of the weak and the taking away from the poor even what they had. Such gods give a quicker reassurance than One who had to teach again and again that the nation was not an ultimate good, and that its existence was secure only insofar as it served an inclusive righteousness and witnessed to a transcendant morality. That often meant that its territorial rights and its rulers' authority could and should be placed at risk for the sake of God's ultimate purposes.

What had to make the longings, and therefore the prayers, of this new people different was that they were not permitted to identify (in any final sense) the object of their longing with anything they already knew or possessed. Their God was unknown, not in the mere sense of being incomprehensible to the reasoning mind, but in the more profound sense of having purposes in mind and gifts to bestow that were always beyond any sign of them that might yet have been discovered. So any 'answers' to prayer that God might offer always contained challenges and promises to do with possibilities yet unknown.

The 'may your reign come, your will be done' which the followers of Jesus were taught to pray is not therefore a shorthand summary of some list that could be made of what would meet our needs or satisfy our desires. Those words stand for the fact that the God to whom we pray is not concerned simply to carry out our wishes in a way that corresponds with any list of things we might imagine, let alone know; rather God responds by shedding abroad on the world a free and unconstrained mercy. So we desire, and in those given words ask for, what we could not describe. And we acknowledge at the same time that what we could describe is too limited by our experience and our insecurity to be as all-embracing as God desires to be.

How that came to be described is as the prayer of those whom God has adopted as God's own children; in words already quoted from St Paul:

> For all who are moved by the Spirit of God are sons of God. The Spirit you have received is not a spirit of slavery leading you back into a life of fear, but a Spirit of adoption, enabling us to cry 'Abba! Father!' In that cry the Spirit of God joins with our spirit in testifying that we are God's children; and if children then heirs. We are God's heirs and Christ's fellow-heirs, if we share his sufferings now in order to share his splendour hereafter. (Rom. 8.14–17)

The very arbitrariness and freedom that adoption involves are the signal that there is mercy yet to give, that we have no exclusive hold on the particular love we have experienced, a love we did not arrive at by nature or merit by our achievement or virtue. There is a toughness to the receiving of the gift and a different, but no less demanding, toughness in watching others receive it for an equal lack of evident reason. But the prayer of the Christian believer acknowledges that the situation which the language of adoption describes is in fact our situation, and that the prayer we offer in the light of that situation always holds that new and unimagined futures are possible.

The power of such adoption language lies also in the fact that it describes more than the situation of those who call themselves believers. By implication it also describes what is basically true about the whole universe of people and things; again, as we have already heard, they also are heard to pray the universal longings of the adopted:

> For I reckon that the sufferings we now endure bear no comparison with the splendour, as yet unrevealed, which is in store for us. For the created universe waits with eager expectation for God's sons to be revealed. It was made the victim of frustration, not by its own choice, but because of him who made it so; yet always there was hope, because the universe itself is to be freed from the shackles of mortality and enter upon the liberty and splendour of the children of God. Up to the present, we know, the whole created universe groans in all its parts as if in the pangs of childbirth. Not only so, but we, to whom the Spirit is given as firstfruits of the harvest to come, are groaning inwardly while we wait for God to adopt us and set our whole body free. (Rom. 8.18–23 NEB, *translation slightly amended*)

Prayer has always to struggle with the arbitrariness, grievances, jealousies and moments of threat to which it gives rise. The times of anger are no less inevitable than the occasions of delight and thankfulness; because the God to whom we pray is the only God there is, because God's mercy is there only as gift and never as reward or entitlement. If we struggle honestly to come to terms with that arbitrariness in prayer, we may be less prone to act out our angry protests in the destructive tribalisms that have been the concern of this book and which are not just the Church's, but humanity's greatest danger.

A Church founded on unmerited and unconstrained mercy may not at times be the Church we would like; but it is the only Church we have been given. It may fail to guarantee our proud entitlements or protect our vulnerabilities; but it is the only kind of Church that could make space for the new life, the rejected perceptions or the unexpected love on which our shared future depends. Above all, it is the kind of Church there would have to be if God really means to love the unwanted more than those whom human structures of power would reward, the only kind of Church that could carry the life that comes from the Cross.

Such, then, is the belonging we have in God. The moments when we experience it, and know ourselves held in that love, are also times when we know there is more to desire, more than we could name.

It is a belonging held open to a universe whose splendour is still to be disclosed. It asks of us that we recognize that what we have desired and experienced may also appear in the lives of our sisters and brothers in ways that are full of surprise and disturbance and which we nevertheless can welcome as promises fulfilled.

Sometimes we may feel required to resist what seems to have no place within the promises of God; but mostly, if the Church's experience is anything to go by, we are more in danger of failing to recognize new beauty and new truth because it comes in unfamiliar guise. And sometimes—if we are like our earliest forebears in the faith it will be quite often—we shall be aware of something we can only describe in Paul's language as the pangs of childbirth, a longing that soon the undisclosed splendour may be revealed. That is how it is when the Spirit prays with our spirit for the revealing of all God's children to be complete.